SHOT MYSTERIES

松濤館の謎

SHOTOKAN MYSTERIES

松濤館の謎

THE HIDDEN ANSWERS TO THE SECRETS OF SHOTOKAN KARATE

KOUSAKU YOKOTA

横田耕作

This book was printed in the United States of America.

To order additional copies of this book, contact:

Azami Press

1-765-242-7988

www.AzamiPress.com

Info@AzamiPress.com

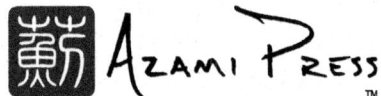

AZAMI PRESS
™

Nazo: 'Mysteries'

DEDICATION
奉納

I dedicate this book to the memory of my parents:

Father, Kimio Yokota (1916–2001)
Mother, Fujiko Yokota (1922–2010)

They gave me a healthy body and taught me honor and pride.

KOUSAKU YOKOTA BIOGRAPHY
経歴

Shihan Kousaku Yokota (横田耕作), eighth *dan*, is a professional *karateka* with extensive experience in various martial arts. With over fifty years of training in Shotokan karate (松濤館空手), he specializes in Asai Ryu Bujutsu karate (浅井流武術空手). His wide range of experience includes training in *kobudo* (*nanasetsukon* and nunchaku), in the art of ki, and in the breathing method by Nishino Ryu Kikojutsu (西野流気功術). He was a member of the JKA for forty years and then joined the JKS for seven years. In 2013, he founded his organization, ASAI (Asai Shotokan Association International [www.asaikarate.com]) to honor Master Tetsuhiko Asai (浅井哲彦). Shihan Yokota travels extensively around the world to share the knowledge and techniques of Asai Ryu karate. He is also a main contributor at Karate Coaching (www.karatecoaching.com), where he extends his karate teaching through Internet media.

ACKNOWLEDGMENTS
感謝の言葉

Once again, many people are responsible for making the creation of this second book, *Shotokan Mysteries*, possible. I want to extend my gratitude to all those who have so generously contributed their time and experience to the creation of this book and to all those who have purchased it.

I dedicate this book to my parents, who are no longer with us in this world. I want to thank them for giving me life and an unbelievably healthy body. I have never seen a doctor or been in a hospital for being sick. They also taught me to be independent and proud. I also want to thank the cultural heritage of Japan and of Shotokan *karatedo* as these taught me honor and respect.

A word of appreciation is due Phillip Kim, who helped me with the creation of the cover for my first book, *Shotokan Myths*, and again for this book.

Bev Yu, Guy Coulston, Mary Boochever, and Tim Ryan were kind enough to do the tedious proofreading of my poor writing in the first edition. Azami Press did an excellent job of further improving the English and content integrity in the second edition.

I would like to give my sincere thanks to all my instructors and students, past and present, for giving me the understanding and knowledge of this great karate style of Shotokan. As Master Funakoshi said, "Karate training is a lifetime endeavor." I am still training and learning every day, yet I have not seen the summit of karate. In the past, I learned from my sensei and my *senpai*. Today, though my sensei have passed, my students and other *karateka* are my new teachers. Without all of you, my karate would not be where it is today, and this book would probably not have materialized.

I also want to thank you, the reader of this book. I hope you enjoy reading it as much as I have enjoyed writing it. I also hope that I get to meet you and train with you in the future. True enjoyment of karate is found in doing it. I dream of a day when all Shotokan practitioners can train together without worrying about politics.

On that day, Funakoshi Sensei and Asai Sensei will be truly pleased.

From the bottom of my heart, I want to say, "Thank you very much to all of you."

皆様に心より御礼申し上げます。

Minasama ni kokoro yori orei mōshiagemasu.

FOREWORD

By Andrew JM Nightingale

Rokudan & Shihankai Member, ASAI

Country Representative, ASAI UK

United Kingdom

If you are the owner or reader of this book, *Shotokan Mysteries* (second edition), you will already be, as I am, a follower and supporter of Yokota Kousaku's work. We, as a worldwide community, are fortunate to have been given such an original and genuine perspective, looking factually from the inside out of the Japanese culture and the structure which surrounds the practice of karate. The various chapters and topics of this book offer martial artists the opportunity to learn and understand much more about karate, explaining many misconceptions surrounding the mysteries of karate, paving the way to a better understanding, and leaving us the choice of change and invaluable additions and insights to improving and refining how and what we already do. The techniques and viewpoints shared through this transcript are a valuable addition to anyone's library, at whatever level you are.

Shotokan Mysteries communicates Yokota Kousaku's work and research into the great, deep golden chest of our continued rediscovery of Shotokan karate in a positive and reflective approach. This book reaches out, openly guiding the reader into recognizing karate as a whole thing itself, paving the way to allow for questions and the subsequent answers to run side by side in a noncritical way, and transcending any misinterpretation or misunderstanding in practice and cultural relationships to the topics and chapters contained within its pages. As the title suggests, the aim of the book is to clear up and correct many collective myths about Shotokan karate which have been allowed to transpire and manifest over the course of time because others refused to share information, couldn't transfer the information through their teaching of karate at a level of deeper understanding, or simply didn't know and created a smoke-and-mirrors approach, hiding facts and information in many guises, with these eventually evolving into mysteries, Shotokan mysteries, in fact! In my opinion, this general lack of knowledge and understanding surrounding Shotokan karate, partnered with the insular thinking of many *karateka*, has only resulted in opening up the position Yokota Shihan respectfully, without malice or arrogance, takes up. It is a position that has sat empty for so long and a position he openly occupies until someone else comes along, in turn, to take up from where he modestly leaves it.

Of course, Yokota's work and research aren't just directed at the Shotokan community. They can be easily accessed and applied to all areas of training within the martial arts genre. He does this by simply describing that a lack of knowledge can be easily changed by challenging and changing your own personal understanding, taking down the boundaries of stuck thought and what is termed far too often as "right and wrong," and dispelling the myths which surround our shared art. The information, in whatever form Yokota puts it forward, transfers to the collective minds of those who share our common passion and is routinely communicated in such a straightforward way that it allows absolutely anyone from any culture or walk of life to understand better and at a higher level the martial art which they have chosen to do. This he does with *Shotokan Mysteries* along with his other books, *Shotokan Myths* and *Shotokan Transcendence*, always with humility, displaying a continuous spirit and correctness reflected in his lifelong practice of *karatedo*.

This reprint of *Shotokan Mysteries* only compounds the necessity of Yokota's continuing work and reflects his continuing rising popularity, especially in the Western world, where we sometimes can become counterproductive in both the advancement of *karatedo* and the perception of the philosophy of the correct mindset for practicing *budo*.

One of the things I personally admire and respect (and have been privy to on many occasions) is the way that Yokota Shihan will always question himself and his own knowledge first and will also always be forthcoming when he has learned something new, stating that we never stop learning and only strive to better practice. Yokota Shihan has quite openly expressed that he wishes that his use of the English language were better in order to properly express himself. If that were so,

I feel that he wouldn't be able to reach out to so many individuals because keeping his language simple and clear adds toward what he intends, which is to try and reach out to as many interested practitioners of karate as possible, helping them to understand their fundamentals and identify where these fundamentals actually sit functionally, practically, and personally. I have tried to write this foreword in the same clear and simple language to reflect upon and show respect to not only Yokota Shihan himself but also to the way which he should continue, which I hope and believe he will do.

There have already been many great pieces written about Yokota Shihan and *Shotokan Mysteries* (first edition) by many reputable individuals, and I am honored by the fact that I was asked to write this foreword for the second edition. Thank you. It is difficult to follow what has already gone before. It was a great surprise and a very difficult thing to apply myself to as so much has already been written. My intention, as a Western *karateka* who has been practicing for more than thirty years, is not to try and communicate to the reader what is in this book because you are about to embark on the reading of it, and your journey through it will be your own. Nor is it to communicate why you should read it because, again, you are about to do so, and, when you start, I can guarantee you will only want to continue and perhaps change a perspective or two and start to question what, how, and why you do what you do, which will only lead you to be better in more ways than one. Isn't that something we all strive for in the short time we have to practice karate? Hopefully, in that time, we are able to inspire others to do the same, only better.

FOREWORD

By Leland Vandervort

Sandan, JKA France

Paris, France

Yokota Kousaku Shihan est un formidable représentant des arts martiaux et plus particulièrement du karaté Shotokan, avec plus de quarante ans de pratique et d'enseignement. Il prend en compte non seulement la technique, mais il met au tout premier rang de son enseignement les résonnances historiques et philosophiques du karaté comme bases de son enseignement. Au-delà de la simple analyse de l'action, en donnant des points de vue différents de la technique, il ouvre ainsi la voie vers une recherche intérieure des applications alternatives plus poussées des techniques de *kata*.

Dans son livre *Shotokan Myths*, Yokota Shihan mettait en lumière des techniques et applications que beaucoup de maîtres de karaté ont cherché à garder secrètes pendant des décennies, et permettait au lecteur de découvrir ces concepts inédits afin de l'aider dans sa recherche personnelle.

Dans cette nouvelle étude, *Shotokan Mysteries*, Yokota Shihan explore et délivre, au-delà de la technique, des questions essentielles de notre pratique du karaté et à partir de cette nouvelle étape, soulève de nouvelles questions.

English

Yokota Kousaku Shihan is a formidable proponent of the martial arts, especially of Shotokan karate, with more than forty years of practice and instruction. He not only takes into account the technique but also places the historical and philosophical aspects of karate at the forefront as the basis of his teaching. Beyond the simple analysis of the action, in giving different viewpoints for the technique, he opens the way for an in-depth search for further alternative applications for the techniques of the *kata*.

In his book *Shotokan Myths*, Yokota Shihan exposed techniques and applications that many karate masters sought to keep secret for decades and allowed the reader to discover these new concepts in order to help in his personal research.

In this new work, *Shotokan Mysteries*, Yokota Shihan explores beyond technique, puts forth essential issues about our karate practice, and, from this new stage, raises new questions.

FOREWORD

By Marcus Hinschberger

JKA Sandan

President & Founder, Karate Coaching

Sacramento, California

Sich selbst in Frage zu stellen und „sein eigenes Glas halb leer zu lassen für neues Wissen", dieser Gedanke ist Teil der Zen-Philosophie (Shoshin - sich den Geist eines Anfängers bewahren).

Jeder *Karateka*, der *Karatedo* wahrhaftig begreifen will, sollte diesem Weg folgen.

In der oft recht „dogmatischen" Karateszene ist Yokota Shihan einer der wenigen Großmeister, der eigenständige Trainings- und Denkansätze vertritt, Überliefertes zu hinterfragen wagt und seine Schüler zu selbständigem Suchen, Forschen und Ausprobieren anhält.

Der tägliche Karate-Trainingsablauf wird durch Yokota Shihan's Trainingsansätze und seine spezielle Herangehensweise aufgebrochen und erfrischend neu gestaltet.

Er ermuntert seine Schüler und Freunde, sich dieser Haltung anzuschliessen und eigenen Ideen, Vorstellungen und Denkansätzen unbedingt zu folgen.

Als Mensch, Lehrer und Vorbild ist Yokota Shihan bescheiden, freundlich und absolut ehrlich.

Seine Lehrgänge bieten einen erfrischend neuen Zugang zu Karate, seine Bücher zeigen längst in Vergessenheit geratene oder noch verborgene Ansätze und Ideen des Karate. Seine Beiträge, wie z.B. im Blog von www.karatecoaching.com, sind provokativ, interaktiv und ermuntern zum freimütigen Gedanken- und Erfahrungsaustausch.

Sich Yokota Shihan anzuschliessen, führt daher unweigerlich zur Begegnung und Auseinandersetzung mit neuen Ideen, einer tieferen Einsicht in *Karatedo*, die *Kata*, das *Bunkai* und erweitert den Einblick in die Geschichte des Karate.

Ich kann Yokota Shihan's Bücher nicht nur empfehlen, sondern ermuntere jeden *Karateka* geradezu, den Kontakt mit diesem Großmeister zu suchen. Die Kommunikation mit ihm wirkt stets inspirierend und endet vielleicht sogar in einer echten Schüler/Meister Bindung.

Ich bin überzeugt, dass der Leser dieses Buch mit großem Interesse lesen wird. Viel Spass bei der Lektüre!

English

John F. Kennedy once said, "Too often...we enjoy the comfort of opinion without the discomfort of thought." This statement is very true for what has been going on within the karate world for decades now. Unfortunately, people tend to prefer dogma over perspective thinking and questioning. This is evident within the karate realm, as well, and has left us with not only many highly dubious *bunkai* applications and explanations but also questionable behavior by some instructors, watered-down competition, and more and more loss of *budo*, which is the essence of karate.

In this world of masters, grand masters, and grand-grand masters, Yokota Shihan is one of the very few who dare to think for themselves, encourage their own students and followers to think for themselves, and be willing not only to question but also to break up dogmatic beliefs. At the same time, he manages to stay humble, approachable, and honest.

His seminars offer a fresh point of view, his books reveal lost or hidden ideas, and his blog posts (at www.karatecoaching.com, for example) are interactive, engaging, and thought provoking for the readers. Following Yokota Shihan will lead you to a wider perspective in your karate beliefs about certain techniques, *kata*, *kata* application, or even karate history and politics, thus deepening your insight into what you already know about karate. Questioning oneself and "keeping the glass empty" is part of Zen—the beginner's mind (*shoshin* [初心])—and every *karateka* who truly wants to understand *karatedo* must travel this path. I cannot only recommend Yokota Shihan's writings but I also want to encourage all *kara-*

teka around the world to seek to contact him. Communicating with and following him will be inspirational and, not surprisingly, may lead to a lasting student-sensei relationship.

I am sure you will enjoy this book.

FOREWORD

By Samir Berardo

Goju Ryu & Shotokan Practitioner

President, ASAI Brazil

Belem, Brazil

Além de um grande artista marcial, Yokota Kousaku Sensei possui raras qualidades entre os autores e pesquisadores de karate de todo o mundo. Esse destaque deve-se à sua extraordinária disposição e mente aberta para obter novas informações, ao seu foco na compreensão do karate enquanto método eficaz de luta, e, finalmente, à coragem de expor ao público ideias fundamentais que muitos ignoraram, alguns imaginaram, e pouquíssimos estiveram dispostos a pronunciar.

A coragem de Yokota Sensei, desafiando intelectualmente interpretações equivocadas e mesmo dogmas que se sedimentaram no mundo do karate moderno e do Shotokan, expressa-se também na disposição de ir contra a tendência contemporânea do excessivo foco esportivo do estilo. Em vez disso, Yokota Sensei reaproxima-o das raízes da arte—o karate enquanto *bujutsu* (arte do guerreiro). Isso combina com o perfil de Yokota Sensei enquanto artista marcial. Até hoje ele conserva um formidável desempenho físico, alcançado por pouquíssimos *karateka* na história, mesmo agora que se aproxima de completar sete décadas de vida. O que se nota é que Yokota Sensei, um *karateka* sempre pronto para utilizar suas habilidades, pratica exatamente aquilo que defende.

Shotokan Mysteries foi escrito por essa personalidade—estudioso, praticante incansável e ainda um veterano que recebeu instrução de grandes nomes do Shotokan, como Jun Sugano e Tetsuhiko Asai. Assim, não é surpresa constatar que este livro constitui uma excelente continuidade à iniciativa do título anterior (*Shotokan Myths*) do autor, buscando desvendar a profundidade e complexidade deste notável estilo e do karate como um todo, tanto nos aspectos históricos quanto no aspecto técnico.

Shotokan Mysteries, que eu tive a felicidade de ler logo após o lançamento da primeira edição, apresenta não só novas informações, mas também o estímulo irresistível para que o leitor passe a olhar o karate de uma maneira diferente—com um olhar mais crítico, e também com uma percepção mais profunda, versátil e eficaz. Ao mesmo tempo em que Yokota Sensei dedica-se à compreensão dos mais profundos aspectos do karate enquanto técnica marcial, percebe-se também em *Shotokan Mysteries* uma preocupação em destacar a importância da arte enquanto caminho de vida e de conduta moral. Esse aspecto é plenamente compreensível ao observar-se a fidelidade devotada pelo autor aos ensinamentos e ao exemplo do mestre que provavelmente foi a sua maior influência, Tetsuhiko Asai.

Finalmente, diante disso tudo percebe-se que uma das características de Yokota Sensei é que ele está sempre evoluindo, até mesmo neste momento avançado de sua extensa carreira de karate. Ele sempre adquire novos conhecimentos e apura ainda mais a sua técnica. Da mesma maneira, acredito que *Shotokan Mysteries* representou, também, uma evolução na sua produção literária, na forma de um livro que complementou e conseguiu ser tão marcante ou mais do que o livro anterior (também obrigatório para praticantes de Shotokan e extremamente recomendado aos *karateka* em geral). Assim, esta segunda edição de *Shotokan Mysteries* representa um verdadeiro refinamento dessa evolução.

English

Beyond being a great martial artist, Yokota Kousaku Sensei has rare qualities among karate authors and researchers around the world. This highlight is due to his extraordinary inclination and open-mindedness toward obtaining new information, his focus on understanding karate as an effective fighting method, and, finally, his courage in showing the public fundamental ideas that many have ignored, some have imagined, and very few have dared to speak of.

The courage of Yokota Sensei, intellectually challenging misconceived interpretations and even dogma that have been settled in modern karate and the Shotokan world, is also expressed in his willingness to go against the contemporary trend of excessive focus on sport within the style. Instead, Yokota Sensei gets closer to the origins of the art—karate as *bujutsu* (the art of the warrior). This combines with Yokota's profile as a martial artist. To this very day, he keeps a formidable physical performance, attained by very few *karateka* in history, even as he now approaches the completion of seven decades of life. It can be clearly noted that Yokota Sensei, a *karateka* always ready to use his abilities, practices exactly what he professes.

Shotokan Mysteries was written by this personality—a scholar, an indefatigable practitioner, and also a senior who received instruction from the great names of Shotokan, such as Jun Sugano and Tetsuhiko Asai. Thus, it is no surprise to find that this book constitutes an excellent continuation by the author of the initiative of the previous title (*Shotokan Myths*), which seeks to unveil the depth and complexities of this remarkable style, and of karate as a whole, in both historical and technical aspects.

Shotokan Mysteries, which I had the good fortune of reading soon after the release of its first edition, presents not only new information but also the irresistible invitation for the reader to begin to look at karate in a different way—with a more critical eye and also with a deeper, more versatile and efficient perception.

At the same time that Yokota Sensei dedicates himself to the understanding of the deepest aspects of karate as a martial technique, one can also perceive in *Shotokan Mysteries* a great interest in highlighting the importance of the art as a way of life and of moral conduct. This aspect is fully comprehended by observing the loyalty devoted by the author to the teachings and example of the master who was probably his greatest influence, Tetsuhiko Asai.

Finally, all of this considered, it can be noted that one of Yokota Sensei's personal traits is the fact that he is always evolving, even at this advanced stage of his extensive karate career. He always acquires new knowledge and hones his technique to higher levels. In the same way, I believe *Shotokan Mysteries* also represents an evolution in his literary production in the form of a book which complements and manages to be just as much or even more remarkable than the previous book by him (also mandatory for Shotokan practitioners and extremely recommended for *karateka* in general). Thus, this second edition of *Shotokan Mysteries* also represents an actual refinement of such an evolution.

FOREWORD

By Oleg Syrel

Sandan, ASAI

Russia

Мне выпала честь быть учеником сенсея Йокоты начиная с фиолетового пояса. Благодаря этой уникальной возможности, многие «Загадки Шотокан» были открыты мне моим сенсеем за годы тренировок, и одним из важных его уроков было то, что человеку, всерьез занимающемуся карате, а в особенности инструктору, знать «как» недостаточно; необходимо понимать, «почему».

«Загадки Шотокан» приглашают читателя понаблюдать вместе с мастером за тем, как классические элементы техники Шотокан изменялись с течением времени, проанализировать причины этих изменений, а так же поразмышлять о том, что мы, изучающие искусство карате, можем сделать для того, чтобы сохранить дух будо, заложенный в его основу. Именно поэтому, помимо технических аспектов Шотокан, сенсей Йокота обсуждает философские и моральные принципы, которыми современное спортивное карате зачастую пренебрегает.

В книге, которую вы держите в руках, сенсей Йокота отвечает на вопросы о том, почему мы тренируемся так, а не иначе, и как мы можем сделать наши занятия карате более осмысленными. Однако, самый важный урок сенсея заключен в примерах того, как нужно задавать вопросы и самим искать на них ответы.

English

I've had the privilege of being Yokota Sensei's student since I was a purple belt. This created the unique opportunity to have many of the Shotokan mysteries uncovered for me by my sensei over the years in the dojo, and one of the important lessons I've learned from his teachings is that, for a serious karate practitioner, and especially for an instructor, knowing why is just as important as knowing how.

Shotokan Mysteries offers an in-depth look by a karate master at how some of the ubiquitous Shotokan techniques evolved over time, what factors influenced the changes, and what we, as karate practitioners, can do to preserve the original *budo* spirit of the art. For this reason, Yokota Sensei goes beyond technique and discusses philosophical and moral principles that are often neglected in the modern, competition-oriented practice of karate.

In the book you're holding in your hands, Yokota Sensei answers questions about why we practice Shotokan karate the way we do and how our karate can be improved to become more meaningful. But, most importantly, through his insightful examples, Sensei teaches us to ask our own questions and seek the answers.

FOREWORD

By Roberto Eisenmann III

Shotokan Practitioner & Close Friend

President, ASAI Panama (2010–2012)

Panama City, Panama

Contados son en el mundo que nos ha tocado vivir quienes, aun al haber llegado a la cima, mantienen su cabeza en posición regular y hasta con una ligera inclinación hacia abajo. Si miran hacia arriba, es para continuar buscando aprender y perfeccionarse y para agradecer a Dios, jamás por arrogancia. Miran hacia abajo, pues la humildad es parte intrínseca de su ser.

El karate debe ser el arte que nos lleva, en la vida real, a enfrentar las vicisitudes con tenacidad y determinación, a evitar confrontaciones, a ser nobles en ves de agresivos, a respetar a los demás. El karate nos debe reforzar el carácter y el alma.

Encuentro del todo sublime haber tenido el privilegio de encontrarme en el camino a alguien que, además de haber nacido en un sitio privilegiado por sus costumbres ancestrales en torno a los valores antes aludidos, vive su vida y el karate como una sola. En su guía, he encontrado luz, serenidad, alivio, fe y esperanza. Mas allá de lo técnico, el fortalecimiento espiritual fundamentado en una filosofía sencilla y de un enaltecimiento exquisito se hace relevante en el verdadero camino del *budo*.

Su primer libro, *Shotokan Myths*, es digno de formar parte de la biblioteca personal de cualquier legítimo artista marcial y/o dojo para leerse a través del tiempo varias veces; este segundo, aun más.

Levanto una taza hecha en hierro forjado, rellena de té verde japonés, y me inclino con merecido respeto y humildad ante la majestuosidad del Maestro Yokota.

English

In the world that we have had to live in, there are very few who, upon reaching the summit, keep their head in a normal position and even with a slight downward tilt. If they do look up, it's to continue to seek to learn and improve themselves and to thank God, never out of arrogance. They look downward for humility is an intrinsic part of their being.

Karate should be the art that helps us, in real life, to face hardships with tenacity and determination, to avoid confrontations, to be noble rather than aggressive, to respect others. Karate should strengthen our character and our soul.

I find it quite sublime to have had the privilege of coming across someone who, in addition to being born in a place privileged by its ancestral customs based on the aforementioned values, lives his life and karate as one. Under his guidance, I have found light, serenity, relief, faith, and hope. Beyond the technical aspect, spiritual strengthening founded on a simple and exquisitely praiseworthy philosophy is made relevant in the true path of *budo*.

His first book, *Shotokan Myths*, is worthy of being a part of any legitimate martial artist's and/or dojo's personal library to be read over the years at various times; this second one, even more so.

I lift a cast-iron cup filled with Japanese green tea and bow with well-deserved respect and humility before Master Yokota's majesty.

松濤館

PREFACE
初めに

Master Gichin Funakoshi, Founder, Shotokan Karate
(1868–1957)

My first book, *Shotokan Myths*, was published in 2010, and, to my great pleasure, it has received a lot of positive feedback from many readers. Some have sent me e-mails and told me that that book gave them a different perspective in their training. One called it her karate bible, which almost embarrassed me, but I felt very honored.

These readers realized there were many "facts" and "truths" that were hidden or taken for granted, and these subjects needed to be questioned. They said that what I shared in that book made sense. I would like to take this opportunity to thank all the readers who have taken the time to read my first book as well as those who have purchased this book.

I cannot believe that three years has already passed since the publication of first edition of this book. I knew that it needed many updates and corrections and wanted to do this much sooner, but it took these three years to get it done. Therefore, I am truly happy that I was finally able to publish the second edition of *Shotokan Mysteries*.

During my early years of training, I was like those readers who wrote and shared their karate lives with me. I was a diligent and blindly dedicated student, so I never questioned anything. When a sensei said, "Jump," I said, "How high?" Of course, the only answer we could give to a sensei in Japan was "*Osu!*"

As I got older, I started to have my own students, and then many questions came to my mind. But, I had no place to go nor anyone knowledgeable to ask to get the answers, so I had to do my own investigation and research.

For the first time, I started to look into the history of Okinawan karate as well as the teachings of other styles. My interest expanded beyond karate, and my research went into ki and various Chinese martial arts. I also bought many books on sports medicine, sports coaching and training theories, and kinesiology as I needed to first understand the mechanics of our mind and body in order to understand what we do with our body and how we do it.

It took me more than ten years of heavy reading and studying, but it was a very interesting journey. It was shocking how I felt after the research, but I must confess that the more I learned, the less confident I became in the general teaching of Shotokan karate that we find in most of the dojo around the world. In fact, in many dojo, it is taught completely incorrectly when you consider the mechanics of our mind and body.

But, even if the common beliefs we learn in a typical dojo happen to be wrong, no one doubts them. I have found that dedicated Shotokan practitioners tend to blindly believe what they are taught by their sensei. Surprisingly, there are many subjects and topics that are almost taboo to discuss. The practitioners are afraid to even look at them.

Many readers have asked me why they have never heard of me before. All through my teaching years, I had flown under the radar or been invisible. I declined all invitations from publications who wanted to write about me, including interviews, and I did not seek out seminars to get exposure.

This attitude, or policy, changed drastically in 2007 for two reasons. One was that my sensei, Tetsuhiko Asai, passed away in 2006, and I felt that I needed to talk about this great master and hand down the techniques that he left us. The other reason was that I turned sixty years old in 2007, and I loved karate too much to keep what I had found all to myself. I felt that I had an obligation to share this with all Shotokan practitioners.

I am happy to have had this opportunity to share my findings and knowledge through this book. I hope what you find here will give you some insight and motivation to train harder to reach the next goal of your karate journey.

Master Tetsuhiko Asai, Founder, Asai Ryu Karate
(1935–2006)

This handwritten letter, dated February 24, 2004, is one of many I received from Master Asai.

CONTENTS

Budo

CHAPTER ONE
第一章

NEW TECHNIQUES BY FUNAKOSHI?
船越の発明?

It is a well-documented fact that Gichin Funakoshi (船越義珍, 1868–1957 [photo left]) was an educator and also a very creative person. He brought many inventions to karate. To name a few, he is known to be the person responsible for switching Heian Shodan and Heian Nidan; he replaced the old *kata* names with more Japanese-sounding names; he invented the *karategi* (空手着, 'karate uniform') and *obi* (帯, 'belt'); and he introduced the *dan* (段) ranking system and the *Dojo Kun* (道場訓). Although the main subject of this chapter is the new techniques he brought in, I would like to further elaborate on these creations.

Chapter 2 discusses the mysteries of the Heian *kata*, and the subject of the switching of Pin'an Shodan (平安初段) and Pin'an Nidan (平安二段) in particular is already included in that chapter, so I will only state here that Funakoshi decided to switch the names because the original Shodan was much more difficult than Nidan. It was his judgment from an educator's point of view that it was better for the novice to learn the current Shodan first. I believe no one disputes this judgment.

He changed many of the *kata* names. For instance, his favorite *kata*, Kanku Dai (観空大), was called *Kosokun* (公相君), *Kusanku* (クーサンクー), or *Kushanku* (クーシャンクー) on Okinawa. Enpi (燕飛) was called *Wansu* (ワンスー) or *Wanshu* (ワンシュー), and Gankaku (岩鶴) was called *Chinto* (チントウ). For Westerners, it really does not matter if a *kata* is called *Kanku* or *Kosokun* as both are foreign words. But, for Funakoshi, it was a bold but necessary move. Once again, although I have written about this in my book *Shotokan Myths*, this subject is extremely important, so I want to reiterate it here.

When Funakoshi brought karate to mainland Japan in the early twentieth century, Okinawa (沖縄) and the Ryukyu Islands (琉球諸島) were barely recognized or known as a part of Japan. In fact, the Ryukyu Kingdom (琉球王国) was an independent country until 1879, when it was formally annexed by the Shimazu Clan (島津氏) of Japan. The Ryukyu Islands were not considered part of Japan, and the Ryukyu people were not considered Japanese. Believe it or not, this prejudice against the Okinawan people continues to the present day.

Funakoshi moved to Japan in 1922, only forty-some years after the annexation, so you can imagine the kind of challenges he had to face. He was not considered to be a true Japanese, and karate was not a Japanese martial art but that of a foreign country with origins that were closer to the Chinese martial arts. And, at that time, Japan was at the height of imperialism and was in conflict with China; thus, anything Chinese was not popular in Japan.

I am sure Funakoshi could speak Japanese, but I imagine he probably had a heavy accent. The culture of Okinawa was also very different from that of Japan; besides the difference in language, even clothing and etiquette varied. In order to get rid of this "foreignness," Funakoshi changed the names of the *kata* to something more "Japanese."

Karate has become very Japanese nowadays, and most Westerners do not doubt that it came from Japan. But, that was not the case at all during the first ten or twenty years after Funakoshi introduced this art into Japan. For karate to be adopted as a Japanese martial art, Funakoshi had to come up with many creative ideas and adjustments (changes), for which we must give him a lot of credit. Without his courageous decisions, karate might not have been adopted by the Japanese at that time, and that could have meant that this art might just have remained a secret martial art of the Okinawans.

Ultimately, this would have meant that there would be no Japan Karate Association (日本空手協会 [JKA]) or Shotokai (松濤會) and no exporting of instructors to the U.S. (Oshima, Nishiyama, Okazaki, Mori, Mikami) or to Europe (Harada, Enoeda, Kase, Shirai, Ochi). Without them, it would be difficult to imagine how karate could have reached its current level of popularity, being practiced and enjoyed by millions of people around the world.

When we think of this now, the change seems to be very natural, but I know that some of the Okinawa masters severely objected to it back then. Their idea was to protect and uphold their tradition, which is also understandable. This was one of the reasons that Funakoshi decided not to return to Okinawa. Even though his wife lived on Okinawa, and they had been separated for many years, he remained in Japan until he passed away in 1957.

His other inventions were the *karategi* and the *dan* ranking system. Jigoro Kano (嘉納治五郎, 1860–1938 [photo left]), the founder of modern-day judo (柔道), was interested in karate. Not only was Kano the owner of the biggest judo dojo in the world at that time, with literally thousands of registered students in Tokyo alone, he was also a school principal as well as an original member of the Olympic committee in Japan. He was a man of power in the Japanese martial arts world who could either help or destroy Funakoshi. So, naturally, Funakoshi adopted some of judo's characteristics into karate.

One of them was to make the *karategi* look almost exactly like the *judogi* (柔道着). He also adopted the belt system and *dan* ranking system just like the way it was done in judo. Funakoshi never claimed any *dan* rank for himself because he was very humble. The *dan* system was a newly developed feature in karate, so by not claiming any rank, he wanted to show the Okinawan masters that he himself had not changed.

I must make note of one important thing that not too many people know or consider important: the one thing that Funakoshi refused to adopt from judo was its sports objective and its *shiai* (試合, 'tournament') system. He proclaimed that karate was *budo* (武道, 'martial art') and did not allow for any tournaments until the day he died.

Funakoshi was the first chairman of the JKA, which was founded in 1949. The

JKA did not have its famous Zenkoku Taikai (全国大会, 'All Japan Champion-ship') until 1957, the very year that Funakoshi passed away. Of course, that was not coincidental. The JKA had to wait until he passed away as they could not get Funakoshi's blessing to hold tournaments. I can sympathize with Funakoshi as I can easily guess that he was frustrated by his wishes to make karate popular yet keep it as a martial art and not a sport.

Another addition to karate training was the recitation of the famous *Dojo Kun*. There are five principles, and I will not get too deep into this as most practitioners are very familiar with them since we repeat them after every training session. I discuss why Funakoshi had to add the *Dojo Kun* to the training menu in Chapter 11: "The Mystery of the Karate Master," where you will see that Funakoshi was a real educator, and he could foresee some potential problems when karate eventu-ally became very popular.

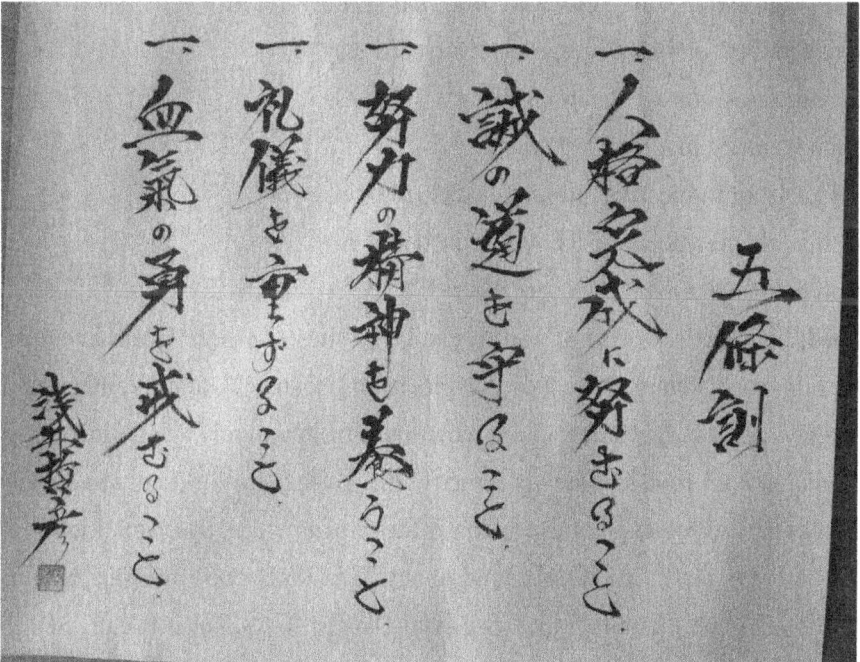

Dojo Kun written by Tetsuhiko Asai

Funakoshi not only made changes to exterior things, such as the *kata* names and the *karategi*, he also ventured into the core and altered Shotokan (松濤館) karate from its original Okinawan form of Shorin Ryu (少林流, 小林流, or 松林流). I wish to cover three distinctive techniques: *yoko geri keage*, *kokutsu dachi*, and *kiai*. Without knowing the background of these techniques and how they came to life, one could view these as mysteries of Shotokan.

Yoko Geri Keage (横蹴り蹴上げ)

In the original Pin'an *kata*, the only kicking techniques found are *mae geri* (前蹴り) and *mikazuki geri* (三日月蹴り). Although *mawashi geri* (回し蹴り) is a popular kick in *kihon* (基本) and *kumite* (組手), it is curious that we do not find it in the Heian *kata*. However, *mikazuki geri*, a kick similar to *mawashi geri*, is a mysterious kick that shows up in Heian Godan (平安五段) despite its rarity in *kihon* and *kumite*.

This is an interesting subject, but I will skip it in this chapter because I cover it in detail in Chapter 4: "Mikazuki Geri, an Extinct Kick?" Instead, here I wish to bring your attention to the *yoko geri keage* in the Heian *kata*. Funakoshi changed the *mae geri* in Heian Nidan and Heian Yondan (平安四段) to *yoko geri keage*. The kicking techniques from not only Pin'an but almost all the original *kata* from Okinawan Shuri Te (首里手) were limited to *mae geri* and *mikazuki geri*. (One distinct exception is the *mawashi geri* and back kick in Unsu [雲手].) *Yoko geri keage* is not found in any *kata*. Only one *yoko geri kekomi* (横蹴り蹴込み) technique is found in Bassai Dai (抜塞大), but it is executed to the *gedan* (下段, 'lower level'), that is, to the knee level.

So, why did he change the *mae geri* to *yoko geri keage*? Is *yoko geri* implemented in the advanced *kata* of Shotokan or Shorin Ryu? Of course it is, and we find it in Bassai Dai and Sho. However, that kick is a *gedan kekomi* (下段蹴込み), and we notice that it is not a high *keage* kick.

But, you may say, "We do *yoko geri keage* in Gankaku and Kanku Dai." Gankaku's original name is *Chinto* and Kanku's is *Kosokun*. Those *kata* are practiced by both Shorin Ryu and Shito Ryu. The techniques in those *kata* are similar, but one big difference is the kicks. Shorin Ryu and Shito Ryu both use *mae geri* instead of *yoko geri keage*. All the kicks in those *kata* are *mae geri*; not a single one is *yoko geri keage*. Shotokan is the only *ryuha* (流派, 'style') that uses *yoko geri keage* in those *kata*. Even Wado Ryu, which branched off from early Funakoshi karate, uses *mae geri* and not *yoko geri keage*. What is the reason for this mystery?

Obviously, Funakoshi changed the kicks in these *kata* from *mae geri* to *yoko geri keage* sometime after Hironori Otsuka (大塚博紀, 1892–1982 [photo right]), the founder of Wado Ryu (和道流), had split from him, which was somewhere between 1929 and 1930. Otsuka started karate training under Funakoshi in 1922 and stayed with him for several years. It is difficult to determine exactly when he split from Funakoshi, but it is well known that Funakoshi and Otsuka did not go their separate ways amicably. (Wado Ryu itself is an interesting *ryuha*, but we will not go into this subject here.)

So, when did Otsuka depart from Funakoshi? Otsuka opened his own dojo in 1931, so we can say that by that time he must have been totally independent and outside of Funakoshi's influence. Therefore, we can assume that Funakoshi changed the kicks from *mae geri* to *yoko geri keage* in all *kata*, including the Heian *kata*, sometime after 1930.

The Okinawan masters had kept the *mae geri* in the *kata* for centuries. It is a big mystery why Funakoshi changed those kicks after he arrived in Japan. I can think of at least two reasons. You must remember that Funakoshi was a dedicated educator, and he was teaching energetic university students. I suspect those young and flexible students asked to learn different kicks. I am sure Funakoshi taught them kicks that were not found in the *kata*, such as *mawashi geri* and *yoko geri keage*. He could explain that *mawashi geri* was a version of *mikazuki geri*—I explain the relationship between these two kicks in Chapter 4—but he had to do something with *yoko geri keage*, so he probably changed some *mae geri* to *yoko geri keage* to create more kicking variety in the *kata*.

In addition, he realized that body shifting is easier when *yoko geri keage* is used. Take Heian Nidan. The seventh move—the same move is found in Kanku Dai—is a right-side *yoko geri keage* toward six o'clock. The sixth move is a right *chudan nobashi zuki* (中段伸ばし突き) toward three o'clock from a right *kokutsu dachi*. If you want to do *mae geri* toward six o'clock, as seen in the original *kata*, you must rotate your body ninety degrees while you are standing on your left leg.

This move is not too difficult for Shorin Ryu and Shito Ryu practitioners. Why? Because, in their *kata*, the stance for the sixth move is *neko ashi dachi* (猫足立ち), a much shorter stance. Thus, it is easier for them to lift the front foot and turn the body ninety degrees. (This is discussed in the next section, "*Kokutsu Dachi*," but Funakoshi also changed *neko ashi dachi* to *kokutsu dachi* in most of the *kata*.) It made sense to Funakoshi to kick with *yoko geri keage* from *kokutsu dachi* without having to change the body's direction.

It is also true that Shotokan *kata* became very dynamic and impressive with the addition of *yoko geri keage*, which is not found in Shorin Ryu or Shito Ryu. Although Funakoshi's son Gigo Funakoshi (船越義豪, 1906–1945) is credited with having adopted high kicks such as *yoko geri keage*—which is not surprising since Gigo was probably more flexible than his father and could execute these techniques better—I believe that Funakoshi Sr. was the one who made the final decision to change.

Nevertheless, unfortunately, this change did result in a couple of negative things: it created a *bunkai* problem, and it caused a loss of an important body rotation movement. On Okinawa there was and still exists, a strict rule to keep all *kata* as they are; no modification or changes are allowed. Because Funakoshi boldly broke this strict rule to make Shotokan *kata* more dynamic and attractive, he was criticized by many Okinawan masters of that time for making too many fundamental changes to Okinawan karate. This was obviously another reason that he never went back to Okinawa. He remained in Japan and lived without his wife until his death at the age of 87.

Kokutsu Dachi (後屈立ち)

You are probably surprised that I call *kokutsu dachi* a mysterious stance. Did you know that Shorin Ryu, the forefather of Shotokan, does not have *kokutsu dachi*? Funakoshi learned the Pin'an *kata* (the original name for the Heian *kata*) on Okinawa with *neko ashi dachi*. Only after immigrating to Japan in the early twentieth century did he change the stance to *kokutsu dachi*. Why did he change it? This is one of the biggest mysteries of Shotokan karate, but not too many people notice or talk about it. I am amazed that all Shotokan practitioners practice this stance diligently without reservation.

The photo to the right shows the fourth move of Shorin Ryu's Pin'an Shodan (Shotokan's Heian Nidan) being performed by a Shorin Ryu practitioner. Shorin Ryu comes from Anko Itosu, the same one who taught Funakoshi. So, we can safely say that very similar moves, including stances, were taught to Funakoshi by Itosu when he was on Okinawa.

Before I go into how *kokutsu dachi* came about, let us look further into the stances of other styles since we can learn some important things from them.

Shorin Ryu does not have a stance called *kokutsu dachi*. They have *neko ashi dachi* instead. However, Shito Ryu and Goju Ryu do have *kokutsu dachi*. What do you think of the stances in the two pictures shown at the top of the following page? Do they look like our *kokutsu dachi*?

Shito Ryu *kokutsu dachi*   Goju Ryu *kokutsu dachi*

No, they look like our *zenkutsu dachi* (前屈立ち) except that the face is turned toward the back as we do in Enpi.

Whether you agree or not, it is a fact that Funakoshi needed to invent this stance after he moved to Tokyo. Neither he nor any of his students documented this invention. I am aware that the findings of my research can be very shocking to many Shotokan practitioners. I expect I will hear many objections and refusals to accept this information, but I dare to reveal this fact for the benefit of keeping Shotokan's history as accurate as possible, and we must know the truth.

Let's take a look at some photos to review this particular stance. The picture shown below is a historic photo that shows Funakoshi leading a group of university students in Heian Nidan (date unknown).

Below is another interesting series of photos showing Funakoshi doing moves four through six of Heian Nidan.

You will notice that the length of this stance is somewhat shorter than what you are taught now. It is almost between the modern-day *kokutsu dachi* and *neko ashi dachi*. Is this because Funakoshi was old and his legs were weak, so his stance was short and high? No, I definitely do not think so. He was in his fifties, and he seems to be in good shape. There must have been another reason. My research shows that Funakoshi had to invent the stance called *kokutsu dachi*.

To answer the question as to why he had to create this stance, we must go back to the challenges Funakoshi faced in Japan, where he had to get support from Kano. Kano had asked Funakoshi to teach some of the former's top students some karate techniques. This was a great opportunity for Funakoshi because he could gain supporters from among the judo practitioners. But, at the same time, it was a risky venture because he could not show that karate was much more lethal than judo or that judo was no match for karate. If the truth were revealed, that is, that judo would be badly beaten by karate, Kano would never support him and his activities, and that would have meant the end of teaching karate in Japan.

In order to get to the inside of an opponent to throw him, the first thing a *judoka* (柔道家) does is grab his lapel and pull him in. How would a *karateka* (空手家) respond? You know that we would immediately kick him in the groin before being grabbed. This is the very purpose of using *neko ashi dachi* when you face an opponent.

Funakoshi could not kick the *judoka* before the latter's hands reached his *karategi* since that would prove that karate's techniques were too lethal and would render judo's first move worthless. Instead, Funakoshi had to pull himself back after he was grabbed. But, since the *judoka* was bigger and stronger, it was not possible for Funakoshi to hold his position in *neko ashi dachi*. Thus, he invented a longer stance to withstand a strong pull, which you can see in the techniques of Heian Yondan. In this scenario, after the struggle, Funakoshi would follow up with a *chudan* (中段, 'middle level') kick.

It may be difficult to believe, but this process was needed to justify a kicking attack. In other words, the *judoka* was given a chance to grab and pull at his opponent first so that he didn't get kicked in the groin from the very beginning. So, Funakoshi decided to change all instances of *neko ashi dachi* in most of the basic *kata* into *kokutsu dachi* and to turn the *neko ashi dachi* followed by a groin kick into a forbidden technique.

Without knowing the tremendous struggle Funakoshi had to go through, the reader may find the following story difficult to believe, but it is a sad truth. Kano was, in fact, so good at marketing judo that Toho Studios made a movie based on the famous judo novel *Sanshiro* (三四郎 [Shun'yodo Shoten, 1909]). A judo expert, Sanshiro, was the main character and the hero. He had an archrival who was a vicious, rude thug. Of course, this rival was a karate practitioner. Funakoshi was supposedly asked to help with the action in the movie that involved karate techniques. Obviously, there was a final showdown at the end of the movie, and you can guess who won.

Thus, the images of viciousness and rudeness portrayed in this movie became the stereotype for all *karateka*, and Funakoshi had to accept this prejudice. But, on the other hand, he gained much acceptance from Kano and his group, which led to his great success in introducing karate into Japan. So, not only did Funakoshi incorporate the *karategi* and the belt-grading concept from judo into karate, he also created a mysterious stance called *kokutsu dachi*.

Kiai (気合)

I have already written on this subject in Chapter 5: "Silent Kiai" of my book *Shotokan Myths*, so I will only give a brief summary here. If you are interested in this subject, I recommend that you read *Shotokan Myths*.

In short, there were no *kiai* in Okinawan karate, especially in the Shuri Te styles, such as Shorin Ryu. Why? Unlike the Naha Te (那覇手) styles, such as Goju Ryu and Uechi Ryu, Shuri Te believed in a natural or quiet breathing method. If a Shuri Te practitioner performed a *kata* with heavy or audible breathing, his performance would be considered poor.

The pre-nineteenth-century masters had to practice in secret. Besides being secretive in general, there were also rivalries among the practitioners themselves. In addition, the Okinawan people were told by the Shimazu Clan not to practice any martial arts at all, which included karate. Therefore, they could only practice in the middle of the night without making any noise. They even had to create a dance with karate techniques in it so that they could lie and say that they were dancing if they were caught in action. So, can you imagine having a loud *kiai* in your *kata* back in those days on Okinawa?

Why did Funakoshi add the *kiai* into karate, then? The *kiai* is considered to be a necessary and important element in Japanese martial arts. It is significant not only in judo but also in kyudo (弓道), jujutsu (柔術), and especially kendo (剣道). I remember that when I was practicing judo, my teacher would tell us that we had to let out a *kiai* every time we threw an opponent. In a tournament, a full point (*ippon* [一本]) would not be awarded unless a throw was accompanied by a loud *kiai*.

So, when Kano sent his students to learn karate from Funakoshi, these judo practitioners must have felt strange training in a very quiet dojo. They felt that the fighting spirit was lacking and suggested that Funakoshi encourage his students to execute the *kiai*. After consideration, Funakoshi decided to adopt it as the young university students must have found an environment filled with loud yells more interesting. I am sure Funakoshi himself held a different belief in *kiai*, but he must have felt he had to make this change.

I mentioned earlier that, originally, *kata* did not have any *kiai*. You can see that some of the Okinawan styles still keep this tradition of having no *kiai* in the *kata*. Funakoshi decided to add two *kiai* to each *kata*, but this was not a strict rule until *kata* was adopted in *shiai* in the late 1950s. Now it is a requirement that competitors deliver at least two loud *kiai* at the "correct" points of the *kata*. Otherwise, points are deducted, which you already know if you are familiar with the current tournament rules.

This is off the subject, but there is another person who turned the *kiai* into a "fashion." If you are a Bruce Lee fan, then you are familiar with his unique *kiai* in his movies. Actually, it became sort of his trademark. He turned the standard "boring" *kiai* into something cool. The Hong Kong kung fu movies they used to produce were boring and oftentimes filled with lots of blood and gore. This was before Jackie Chan and Jet Li. Bruce Lee definitely created a totally new kind of kung fu movie that was very fun and entertaining to watch. His facial expressions and *kiai* were a big part of his success.

Because of the incorporation of the long *kokutsu dachi*, the dynamic *yoko geri keage*, and the loud *kiai*, Shotokan karate, in fact, became quite different from the original Te (手) that Funakoshi brought to Japan in 1922. Whether you consider the changes that Funakoshi made to be good or bad for karate, no one can deny that without Funakoshi's lifelong endeavor involving much patience and diplomacy, this Okinawan art of Te could not have seen such huge success and become one of the major martial arts of Japan.

押
忍

CHAPTER TWO
第二章

THE MYSTERIES OF THE HEIAN KATA
平安形の謎

The Heian *kata* are the fundamental *kata* that make up the backbone of Shotokan karate. These are the first *kata* a white belt learns unless his dojo practices the Taikyoku (太極) series as the first *kata*. How many times have you practiced the Heian *kata*? Maybe you have practiced them several hundreds of times or even more. For some senior practitioners, it might be thousands of times. So, you may feel you know these *kata* like the back of your hand. In this chapter, I will bring up many points that are taken for granted yet, under close scrutiny, appear to be very mysterious. You will be surprised to find the truth and the facts that underlie the history of Shotokan.

Many Shotokan *kata* are believed to be quite old. Some are said to have been around as long as the several-hundred-year-old history of Shuri Te, of which Shotokan is a branch. On the other hand, the fundamental *kata*, Heian Shodan through Godan, were created by one modern-day master of Shuri Te, Anko Itosu (糸洲安恒, 1831–1915 [photo left]), in the late nineteenth century. Some claim the creation date of these *kata* to be during the early twentieth century because karate was introduced into the public school system in 1901. But, for this very reason, I believe the date to be in the late nineteenth century since Itosu must have had to use this *kata* to convince school management that karate training was not only beneficial but also safe for school children.

Before the creation of Heian (originally called *Pin'an* but written with the same characters [平安]), the first *kata* that Shuri Te students learned were the ones in the Tekki (鉄騎) series (originally called *Naihanchi* [ナイハンチ] or *Naifanchi* [ナイファンチ]). Training on Okinawa was conducted secretly inside the master's house or in a graveyard at night. Additionally, an Okinawan sensei typically took on only one or two students at any given time, and a group lesson was unheard of.

As Japan began opening its ports to foreign countries during the Meiji Restoration (*Meiji Ishin* [明治維新]) in the middle of the nineteenth century, which brought about the end of the samurai and feudalism in Japan, the system of royalty on Okinawa was also abandoned. With this big change, karate was no longer needed by the palace guards as there was no longer a king to protect.

Naturally, people weren't exactly knocking down the karate masters' doors to ask for their instruction, and these masters feared that karate would soon be forgotten. In order to save karate, Itosu convinced the government of Okinawa to include it as part of the public school physical education activities. It was formally incorporated into the curriculum of the elementary schools in 1901 and into that of the high schools in 1905. Accordingly, Itosu formulated a teaching syllabus for giving group lessons.

One of the challenging things he had to do was to create a new set of *kata* that was appropriate for the complete novice. In former times, when karate was taught one-to-one, a student was required to do a lot of household chores, such as carrying water and firewood, helping with fieldwork, cleaning the house, etc. During this process, which could last several years, the student did not receive any formal

training or teaching. The student's body was exercised to develop its natural strength.

If the teacher thought the student needed more leg strength, he might make him stand in *kiba dachi* (騎馬立ち) for hours. So, by the time he completed this pretraining period, his legs would be in very good shape. He might see his teacher practicing *kata* and thus could be prepared to take on the first *kata*, Tekki.

We all know that Tekki is a very unique *kata*. The steps are only from side to side, and there is a specific objective to this *kata*. I wrote in depth about this subject in Chapters 9 and 10 of my first book, *Shotokan Myths*, so please refer to those chapters for more detail on this topic.

The essence of Tekki is not appropriate for the student who is a complete novice as the specific study points are quite advanced. Other advanced *kata*, such as Bassai and Kanku, are, of course, too difficult and not appropriate for school children. Thus, Itosu created a set of *kihon kata* (基本形, 'basic forms') called *Pin'an* (now *Heian* in Shotokan), which were much easier for students to learn and for instructors to teach. Pin'an was adopted soon afterward by all Shuri Te organizations, such as Shorin Ryu, Shotokan, Wado Ryu, and even Shito Ryu (a hybrid style of both Shuri Te and Naha Te lineage).

This is a brief history on the background of the Heian series, which many readers already know. The history of this series is a little over a hundred years old, yet, surprisingly, there are many unchecked and strange "facts" found within these *kata*. Some of these are indeed mysteries, but it is stranger still that few have ever questioned or challenged them. I was too curious to be quiet, so I researched the real facts.

There are many unanswered questions in Shotokan karate. I call these subjects *mysteries*. I am happy to present these mysteries here and to share my understanding and hypotheses. I hope this will become a bridge to the answers to these questions and to a better understanding of the Heian *kata*.

Mystery 1: Origin and Channan (チャンナン)

It is well documented that the creator of the Pin'an *kata* is Anko Itosu. He wanted to popularize karate by having it adopted by the public school system. He was the organizer of this movement and with his great work, karate became a part of physical education in elementary schools in 1901 and then in high schools in 1905. It is also documented that Itosu created Pin'an for the school system in the late nineteenth century in order to show this simple *kata* to school officials and to convince them that it could be learned by students who were totally new to karate.

The names *Pin'an* and *Heian* are written with the same Chinese characters. Even though the versions of the Pin'an *kata* handed down by Shorin Ryu and Shito Ryu are slightly different from the version called *Heian*, I am sure the reader will agree that Heian came from Pin'an.

Up to this point, the history of Heian is well documented. We now look further back to try to understand how Itosu created Pin'an. The mystery is where this *kata* came from. Itosu did not leave any written record of this, but students such as Mabuni, Funakoshi, and Motobu mentioned an original *kata* called *Channan*. So, the mystery is this *kata*, Channan. Regarding this unknown *kata*, there are two theories as to its origin. Let us look into each theory.

Theory A: *Channan*, an Old Name for Pin'an

One theory is that *Channan* was the original name of the *kata* Itosu created in honor of a Chinese martial artist who had been shipwrecked on Okinawa and had taught him some Chinese fighting arts. When he introduced this *kata* into the public schools in the early twentieth century, he changed the name to *Pin'an*. It is said that he asked the school students to come up with a new name, and one student came up with the name *Pin'an*, meaning 'peaceful'.

There is an excellent article on Channan by Joe Swift. With his permission, I have reprinted the entire article on this subject below.

Channan: The "Lost" *Kata* of Itosu?

Introduction

The series of five basic *kata* called *Pin'an* (later renamed *Heian* in Japan) are probably the most widely practiced *kata* in karate today. It is commonly understood that they were developed by Anko (or Yasutsune) Itosu (1832–1915) in around 1907 for inclusion in the karate curriculum of the Okinawan school system. However, the actual history of the Pin'an series has been the subject of intense curiosity as of late. There are basically two schools of thought, one that Anko Itosu (1) developed them from the older classical forms that were cultivated in and around the Shuri (capital of Okinawa) area, and the other that Itosu was reworking a longer Chinese form called *Channan.*

Unfortunately, most of the written references to the Channan/Pin'an phenomenon in the English language are basically rehashes of the same uncorroborated oral testimony. This article will examine the primary literature written by direct students of Itosu, as well as more recent research in the Japanese language, in an effort to solve the "mystery" of Channan.

Anko Itosu

In order to understand the Pin'an phenomenon, perhaps it is best to start off with a capsule biography of their architect, Anko Itosu (1832–1915). Many sources state that Itosu was born in the Yamakawa section of Shuri (Bishop, 1999; Okinawa Prefecture, 1994; Okinawa Prefecture, 1995); however, noted Japanese martial arts historian Tsukuo Iwai states that he was actually born in Gibo, Shuri, and later relocated to Yamakawa (Iwai, 1992). He is commonly believed to have studied under Sokon ("Bushi") Matsumura (1809–1901) but also appears to have had other influences, such as Nagahama of Naha (Iwai, 1992; Motobu, 1932), Kosaku Matsumora of Tomari, and a master named *Gusukuma* (Nihon Karate Kenkyukai, 1956).

There does not seem to be much detail about Itosu's early life, except for the fact that he was a student of the Ryukyuan civil fighting traditions. At around age 23, he passed the civil service examinations and was employed by the royal government (Iwai, 1992). It seems as if Itosu gained his position as a clerical scribe for the king through an introduction by his friend and fellow karate master Anko Asato (Funakoshi, 1988). Itosu stayed with the royal government until the Meiji Restoration, when the Ryukyu Kingdom became Okinawa Prefecture. Itosu stayed on and worked for the Okinawan prefectural government until 1885 (Iwai, 1992).

There is some controversy as to when Itosu became a student of Matsumura. Some say that he first met Matsumura when Itosu was in his late 20s (Iwai, 1992), whereas others maintain that Itosu was older than 35 when he began studying from Matsumura (Fujiwara, 1990). Matsumura appears to have been friendly with Itosu's father (Iwai, 1992).

Be that as it may, Itosu is said to have mastered the Naifuanchi *kata* (Nihon Karate Kenkyukai, 1950; Okinawa Pref., 1995). In fact, one direct student of Itosu, namely, Funakoshi Gichin, recalled 10 years of studying nothing but the three Naifuanchi *kata* under the eminent master (Funakoshi, 1976) (2).

Again, there is some controversy as to where Itosu learned the Naifuanchi *kata*. Some give credit to Matsumura for teaching this *kata* to Itosu (Murakami, 1991). However, others say differently, and here is where we first start to see reference to Channan, as the name of a person. It is said that a Chinese sailor who was shipwrecked on Okinawa hid in a cave at Tomari. It was from this man that Itosu supposedly learned the Naifuanchi *kata*, among other things (Gima et al., 1986).

In either case, it is known that Itosu was among the first to teach karate (*toudi*) publicly, karate having previously been taught and practiced in secrecy for hundreds of years. Itosu began his public teaching of karate as physical education in the school system as early as 1901, where he taught at the Shuri Jinjo Primary School (Iwai, 1992; Okinawa Pref., 1994). He also went on to teach at Shuri Dai Ichi Middle School and the Okinawa Prefectural Men's Normal School in 1905 (Bishop, 1999; Okinawa Pref., 1994, 1995).

In addition to his "spearheading a crusade" (McCarthy, 1996) to modernize *toudi* practices and get it taught in the school system, Itosu was also known for his physical strength. It is said that he was able to crush a bamboo stalk in his hands (Funakoshi, 1976, 1988), that he once wrestled a raging bull to the ground and calmed it (Nagamine, 1986), and that one could strike his arms with 2-inch thick poles and he would not budge (Iwai, 1992).

Itosu's unique contributions to the art of *karatedo* include not only his 1908 letter to the Japanese Ministry of Education and Ministry of War (3), expounding on the 10 precepts of *toudi* training, but also the creation of several *kata*. These include not only the Pin'an series, but also Naifuanchi Nidan and Sandan (Kinjo, 1991; Murakami, 1991) and possibly Kusanku Sho and Passai Sho (Iwai, 1992). Another *kata* that has often been attributed to Itosu is the Shiho Kusanku Kata (Kinjo, 1956a; Mabuni et al., 1938), but more recent evidence points to the actual originator of this paradigm as having been Mabuni Kenwa himself (Sells, 1995).

In addition to creating several *kata*, the other *kata* that Itosu taught, such as Chinto, Useishi (Gojushiho), Passai Dai, Kusanku Dai, etc., were changed from their original guises in order to make them more palatable to his physical education classes (Kinjo, 1991).

Anko Itosu passed away in March 1915, leaving behind a legacy that very few today even recognize or comprehend.

Early Written References to Channan and Pin'an

References to Channan can be found as far back as 1934. In the karate research journal entitled *Karate no Kenkyu*, published by Nakasone Genwa, Motobu Choki is quoted referring to the Channan and the Pin'an *kata*:

> *(Sic.) I was interested in the martial arts since I was a child, and studied under many teachers. I studied with Itosu Sensei for 7–8 years. At first, he lived in Urasoe, then moved to Nakashima Oshima in Naha, then on to Shikina, and finally to the villa of Baron Ie. He spent his final years living near the middle school.*
>
> *I visited him one day at his home near the school, where we sat talking about the martial arts and current affairs. While I was there, 2–3 students also dropped by and sat talking with us. Itosu Sensei turned to the students and said, "Show us a* kata.*"*
>
> *The* kata *that they performed was very similar to the Channan* kata *that I knew, but there were some differences also. Upon asking the student what the* kata *was, he replied, 'It is Pin'an no Kata."*
>
> *The students left shortly after that, upon which I turned to Itosu Sensei and said, "I learned a* kata *called Channan, but the* kata *that those students just performed now was different. What is going on?"*
>
> *Itosu Sensei replied, "Yes, the* kata *is slightly different, but the* kata *that you just saw is the* kata *that I have decided upon. The students all told me that the name* Pin'an *is better, so I went along with the opinions of the young people."*
>
> *These* kata, *which were developed by Itosu Sensei, underwent change even during his own lifetime. (Murakami, 1991; 120)*

There is also reference to Pin'an being called *Channan* in its early years in the 1938 publication *Kobo Kenpo Karatedo Nyumon* by Kenwa Mabuni and Genwa Nakasone. Mabuni and Nakasone write that those people who learned this *kata* as *Channan* still taught it under that name (Mabuni et al., 1938).

Hiroshi Kinjo, one of Japan's most senior teachers and historians of the Okinawan fighting traditions and a direct student of three of Itosu's students, namely, Chomo Hanashiro, Chojo Oshiro, and Anbun Tokuda, wrote a series of articles on the Pin'an *kata* in *Gekkan Karatedo* magazine in the mid-1950s. In the first installment he maintains that the Pin'an *kata* were originally called *Channan*, and there were some technical differences between Channan and the updated versions known as *Pin'an* (Kinjo, 1956a).

Again, according to Hiroshi Kinjo, Hisateru Miyagi, a former student of Itosu who graduated from the Okinawa Prefectural Normal School in 1916, stated that when he was studying under the old master, Itosu only really taught the first three Pin'an with any real enthusiasm, and that the last two seem to have been rather neglected at that time (Kinjo, 1956b). Although one can speculate about what this means, it is nevertheless a very interesting piece of testimony by someone who was "there."

Ryusho Sakagami, in his 1978 *Karatedo Kata Taikan*, as well as Tokumasa Miyagi, in his 1987 *Karate no Rekishi*, both give extensive *kata* lists, and both list a *kata* known as *Yoshimura no Channan* (Miyagi, 1987; Sakagami, 1978). It is unknown who Yoshimura was, but he may have been a student of Itosu.

American karate historian Ernest Estrada has also stated that Juhatsu Kyoda (1887–1968), a direct student of Kanryo Higashionna, Wu Xianhui (Jpn., Go Kenki), Kentsu Yabu, etc., and the founder of the To'onryu Karatedo system, also knew and taught a series of two basic blocking, punching, and kicking exercises known as *Channan* (Estrada, 1998).

Shiraguma no Kata

According to Tsukuo Iwai, one of Japan's most noted *budo* researchers and teacher of Choki Motobu's karate in Gunma Prefecture, Motoburyu Karatejutsu, which is being preserved by Choki's son, Chosei Motobu, in Osaka, contains what is known as *Shiraguma no Kata*, which he maintains used to be called *Channan*. He also states that this *kata* is "somewhat similar to the Pin'an, yet different." (Iwai, 1997).

The Other Side of the Coin

The flip side to this theory states that Itosu did not create the Pin'an *kata* but actually remodeled older Chinese-based *hsing/quan/kata* called *Channan*. This theory states that Itosu learned a series of Chinese *quan fa hsing* from a shipwrecked Chinese at Tomari and reworked them into five smaller components, renaming them *Pin'an* because the Chinese pronunciation "Chiang Nan" was too difficult (Bishop, 1999).

It has been argued that the source for these Channan *kata* was a Chinese from an area called *Annan* or a man named *Annan* (Bishop, 1999). On the other hand, others say that the man's name was *Channan* (Iwai, 1992). Still others go into even more detail, stating that Itosu learned these *hsing/kata* from a man named *Channan* and named them after their source, later adding elements of the Kusanku Dai *kata* to create the Pin'an (Gima et al., 1986; Kinjo. 1999).

There is also interesting oral testimony passed down in the Tomaridi tradition that is propagated in the Okinawa Gojuryu Tomaridi Karatedo Association of Iken Tokashiki that states that Itosu learned the Channan/Pin'an *kata* from a Chinese at Tomari in one day. The proponents of Tomaridi said that there was no need to learn "overnight *kata*" and that this is the reason that the Tomari traditions did not include instruction in the Pin'an *kata* (Okinawa Pref., 1995).

This sentiment also echoes the statement by one of Itosu's top students, Yabu Kentsu, made to his students:

(sic) If you have time to practice the Pin'an, practice Kushanku instead (Gima et al., 1986, p. 86).

Conclusion

While more research, such as in-depth technical analysis of Motobu's Shiraguma no Kata, needs to be done, the evidence at hand seems to point not to a "long-lost *kata*" but rather to the constant and inevitable evolution of a martial art.

Although there is opposition, most of the primary written materials point to the fact that Itosu was indeed the originator of the Channan/Pin'an tradition, based upon his own research, experience, and analyses.

However, in either case, Anko Itosu and his efforts left a lasting mark on the fighting traditions of old Okinawa and will probably always be remembered as one of the visionaries who were able to lift the veil of secrecy that once enshrouded *karatedo*.

Notes

1. Japanese names in this article are listed by given name first and family name second instead of customary Japanese usage, which places the family name first.

2. According to noted Japanese martial arts historian Ryozo Fujiwara in his 1990 book entitled *Kakutogi no Rekishi* (*History of the Martial Arts*), Funakoshi first learned Pechurin (Suparinpei) under Taite Kojo, then Kusanku

under Anko Asato, and finally Naifuanchi under Itosu.
3.   For a comprehensive English translation of this letter, see McCarthy, 1990.

Bibliography

Bishop, M. (1999). *Okinawan Karate: Teachers, Styles and Secret Techniques, 2nd Edition*. Boston: Charles E. Tuttle, Co.

Estrada, E. (1998). Personal Communication: Kyoda and Channan.

Fujiwara, R. (1990). *Kakutogi no Rekishi (History of Martial Arts)*. Tokyo: Baseball Magazine.

Funakoshi G. (1976). *Karatedo: My Way of Life*. Tokyo: Kodansha International.

Funakoshi G. (1988). *Karatedo Nyumon*. Tokyo: Kodansha International. Tr. by John Teramoto.

Gima S. and Fujiwara R. (1986). *Taidan: Kindai Karatedo no Rekishi wo Kataru (Talks on the History of Modern Karatedo)*. Tokyo: Baseball Magazine.

Iwai T. (1992). *Koden Ryukyu Karatejutsu (Old-Style Ryukyu Karatejutsu)*. Tokyo: Airyudo.

Iwai T. (1997). Personal Communication: Shiraguma no Kata.

Kinjo A. (1999). *Karate-den Shinroku (True Record of Karate's Transmission)*. Naha: Okinawa Tosho Center.

Kinjo H. (1956a). "Pinan no Kenkyu (Study of Pinan) Part 1." *Gekkan Karatedo* June 1956. Tokyo: Karate Jiho-sha.

Kinjo H. (1956b). "Pinan no Kenkyu (Study of Pinan) Part 2." *Gekkan Karatedo* August 1956. Tokyo: Karate Jiho-sha.

Kinjo H. (1991). *Yomigaeru Dento Karate 1 Kihon (Return to Traditional Karate Vol. 1, Basic Techniques)* (video presentation). Tokyo: Quest, Ltd.

Mabuni K. and Nakasone G. (1938). *Karatedo Nyumon (Introduction to Karatedo)*. Tokyo: Kobukan.

McCarthy, P. (1996). "Capsule History of Koryu Karate." *Koryu Journal* Inaugural Issue. Australia, International Ryukyu Karate Research Society.

McCarthy, P. (1999). *Ancient Okinawan Martial Arts: Koryu Uchinadi, Vol. 2*. Boston: Charles E. Tuttle, Co.

Miyagi T. (1987). *Karate no Rekishi (The History of Karate)*. Naha: Hirugisha.

Motobu C. (1932). *Watashi no Toudijutsu (My Karate)*. Tokyo: Toudi Fukyukai.

Murakami K. (1991). *Karate no Kokoro to Waza (The Spirit and Technique of Karate)*. Tokyo: Shin Jinbutsu Oraisha.

Nagamine S. (1986). *Okinawa no Karate Sumo Meijin Den (Tales of Okinawa's Great Karate and Sumo Masters)*. Tokyo: Shin Jinbutsu Oraisha.

Nihon Karate Kenkyukai (1956). *Zoku: Karatedo Nyumon (Introduction to Karatedo: Continued)*. Tokyo: Wakaba Shobo.

Okinawa Prefecture Board of Education (1994). *Karatedo Kobudo Kihon Chosa Hokokusho (Report of Basic Research on Karatedo and Kobudo)*. Naha: Nansei.

Okinawa Prefecture Board of Education (1995). *Karatedo Kobudo Kihon Chosa Hokokusho II (Report of Basic Research on Karatedo and Kobudo Part II)*. Naha: Nanasei.

Sakagami R. (1978). *Karatedo Kata Taikan (Encyclopedia of Karatedo Kata)*. Tokyo: Nichibosha.

Sells, J. (1995). *Unante: Secrets of Karate*. Hollywood: Hawley

If we believe Itosu was the one who created Channan, then how did he do that? The first theory says Itosu selected some techniques that were not dangerous but were excellent for physical exercise.

It is true that Heian Shodan has a sequence of four *shuto uke* that is also found in Kanku Dai. Heian Nidan has many moves that are identical to those in Kanku Dai, including this sequence. In fact, starting from the right *yoko geri keage* all the way up to the simultaneous left *osae uke* (押さえ受け) and right *chudan nukite* (中段貫手), the moves are identical. Heian Sandan (平安三段) has some techniques that are similar to those in Jion (慈恩) and Gankaku, namely, *enpi uke* (猿臂受け). Heian Godan has many moves that are found in Bassai Dai, Kanku Dai, and Gankaku. To make learning and teaching in middle school easier, he created five short *kata* rather than one long *kata*.

Theory B: Channan, a Model *Kata*

The second theory is that Channan was a much longer *kata* that consisted of two parts (Dai and Sho). According to this theory, Itosu supposedly made five *kata* by taking parts from Channan. One advocate of this theory is Dr. Elmar Schmeisser. His book *Channan: Heart of the Heians* is available through *Amazon*, so you may purchase a copy if you are interested in this theory. One reviewer of his book had this to say about it:

> *Channan: Heart of the Heians*, by Elmar T. Schmeisser, explores the possibility of the modern-day Heians as derived from the Chinese *kata* Channan Dai and Channan Sho. The author makes no definitive claim that his studies are absolute but presents his research in a sound, historical manner, leaving the reader to make his or her own decision regarding the origins of the Heian *kata* based on the research presented. The book is loaded with simple-to-follow, step-by-step photos of Channan Dai and Channan Sho and accompanying text for each step. In a simple, straightforward way, the author clearly illustrates apparent or perceived correlations between the Channan *kata* and the modern-day Heians.
>
> An added plus in this book is the way it is laid out; the book is designed in a way that...flow[s] seamlessly from one photographic illustration to another...This book is a fantastic work and will be greatly appreciated by anyone who enjoys the study of traditional Japanese *kata*, *bunkai*, and *kata* origins.

One thing I need to mention about his research is that he learned this *kata* from an instructor in the Philippines and not from an Okinawan. This *kata* is said to have been handed down from China to Southeast Asia (not Okinawa) and then to the Philippines, where he learned it. Because of this lineage, I tend to think the first theory is more believable than the second one.

Aside from the historical point of view, the author put a lot of effort into the *bunkai* of the *kata*, and I found some to be excellent and useful. So, even if you do not agree with the historical perspective, this book can be a good read for those Shotokan practitioners who like to study the *bunkai* of the Heian *kata*.

It is totally up to the reader to decide which of these two theories is closer to the truth. Much research has been done, and a lot of questions have been answered, but there are many more questions that are still unanswered. Due to the lack of written documents and records on Okinawa, I suspect these questions will never be answered, and I fear that the real stories will disappear into the folds of history.

Mystery 2: Shodan and Nidan

Many readers may already know that Itosu, the creator of Pin'an, set what we call *Heian Nidan* (originally *Pin'an Shodan*) as the first *kata* and what we call *Heian Shodan* (originally *Pin'an Nidan*) as the second *kata*. When Funakoshi introduced the Heian *kata* into Japan, he switched the order of Heian Shodan and Heian Nidan to where we see them now.

Shorin Ryu and Shito Ryu, on the other hand, kept the original order. However, it makes sense to practice Heian Shodan first as it is the simpler *kata* and is much easier than Nidan. The puzzling question is why Itosu put a more challenging *kata* before a much simpler and easier *kata*. I am sure it was intentional, so what was the reason, and what were his intentions?

Funakoshi switched the order of Heian Shodan and Heian Nidan, thus confusing the explanation of the history of Pin'an Shodan/Nidan with regard to Heian Shodan/Nidan. So, I will use the term *Original Shodan* to refer to the original Pin'an Shodan (according to Itosu's order) and the term *Current Shodan* to refer to Shotokan's Heian Shodan (according to Funakoshi's order).

Similarly, the original Pin'an Nidan (according to Itosu's order) will be referred to as *Original Nidan*, and Shotokan's Heian Nidan (according to Funakoshi's order) will be referred to as *Current Nidan*. I hope this method will minimize the possibility of confusion.

It is well known that Shorin Ryu and Shito Ryu kept the original order. By the way, examining Shorin Ryu and Shito Ryu is very useful when studying the origin of Shotokan. Shorin Ryu is Shuri Te and is directly descended from Itosu. Shito Ryu is an interesting style as it is supposed to have elements of both Shuri Te and Naha Te. Kenwa Mabuni (摩文仁賢和, 1889–1952 [photo left]), the founder of this style, learned Shuri Te from Itosu (糸洲) and Naha Te from Higaonna (東恩

納). By taking the first Chinese character from each sensei's family name, i.e., 糸 and 東, Mabuni created the name for his style, Shito Ryu (糸東流).

As I mentioned earlier, Funakoshi was the one who switched the order of these two *kata* after introducing them into Japan, and it is easy to figure out why he switched them. Original Shodan clearly has more challenging techniques, such as its kicks, *gyaku hanmi* (逆半身), and *gyaku zuki* (逆突き). Funakoshi was an educator, and it certainly made sense for him to put the easier *kata* first and then move on to the more challenging *kata*. So, the real question is this: why did Itosu place a more complex *kata*, Original Shodan, before a simpler *kata*, Original Nidan? This was a mystery to me.

I have heard speculation that after Itosu created Original Shodan, he found that novice students had so many problems that he created a simpler *kata*, Original Nidan. I do not agree with this idea. If Itosu had thought Original Nidan was a better *kata* for beginning students, he would have switched the order as Funakoshi did. But, he kept the original order, a fact that shows that his decision to start with Original Shodan was intentional.

Interestingly, Shito Ryu and other Shuri Te styles on Okinawa did not adopt the original order exactly. According to a book written by Mabuni of Shito Ryu, the order of instruction is to teach Original Nidan first and then Sandan before the student is exposed to Original Shodan. The reason for this order can be explained simply by the fact that these two *kata* are easier to teach to beginners than Original Shodan. So the question remains: what were Itosu's intentions in setting up Original Shodan as the first *kata* of the Heian series?

Here is my hypothesis for his intentions and the reason for the *kata* order. It is clearly documented that Itosu was an excellent *karateka* and sensei and that he was the key person who introduced karate into the public education system. However, what is not written is that, I assume, he was an old-school martial artist before he was an educator.

As a traditional Shuri Te sensei with the former one-to-one method of teaching, he wanted to begin with a "real" *kata*, something with high-level techniques that would be similar to a *kata* such as Kosokun (Kanku Dai). It sounds almost contradictory to teach a novice student a difficult *kata*, but I understand how he felt. For him, Original Nidan was too simple and was not good enough to be used as a first *kata*.

Kosokun (Kanku Dai) is the backbone of Shuri Te as it is in Shotokan. As the reader will note, the sequence that runs from the first kick to the *nukite* in Original Shodan is found in Kanku Dai. From that sequence, it goes on to four *shuto uke* techniques, which are also found in Kanku Dai. Original Nidan, on the other hand, has no identical techniques and few—the last four *shuto uke* movements, for example—that are similar to original Shuri Te *kata* such as Kanku, Bassai, and Jion.

I suspect he believed that the first Pin'an *kata* must be similar to the *kata* Kanku Dai. Thus, I conclude that Itosu, the martial artist, sincerely believed that novice students would progress further by learning a "real" *kata* first before moving on to a *kata* that was very basic in its techniques. So, I believe that Itosu was a martial artist first and an educator second.

Funakoshi was with Itosu for many years, so he must have known his sensei's intentions and concepts. So, why did he make a switch that contradicted his sensei's belief, then? This is also a mystery.

I believe there were at least three reasons. One is that Funakoshi was an educator in a broader sense before being a karate instructor of the old Okinawan school. He saw more value in being able to teach more easily than in maintaining the martial arts challenge.

The second and more pressing reason was that he had to teach these *kata* to Japanese university students, who were vastly different from the more mentally prepared Okinawan youth. Funakoshi faced Japanese students who had no concept of karate or its training, and they would practice only four years until graduation. It was impossible to continue karate training after college in Tokyo at that time as there were no karate dojo there. So, he had only four years to teach all those *kata*, starting with Heian.

On Okinawa, a teacher used to expect students to focus on one *kata* for three to five years. If Funakoshi had kept that mentality, it would have taken him fifteen to twenty-five years to teach all the Heian *kata*. If he wanted to produce any *yudan-sha* (有段者, 'black belts'), he would have to teach not only Heian but at least five other *kata*, and he had only four years to do this. You can easily imagine that the process had to be faster for university students, so the ease with which the material could be taught had to take priority.

The third reason is less obvious. Many readers are probably not aware that Funakoshi had the support of Kano, the founder of judo, when he started to teach karate in Tokyo. Kano requested that he teach *kata* to some of his senior students, a request that Funakoshi could not refuse. For judo practitioners, kicks are the most difficult techniques; thus, introducing Current Shodan to judo practitioners made sense.

In addition, you must know that Funakoshi's Japanese was a heavily accented Okinawan dialect, whereas the university students and judo practitioners spoke Tokyo dialect, or Kanto (関東) dialect. Without exaggeration, these two dialects were virtually two totally different languages. A good comparison would be more like the difference between Spanish and Portuguese than the difference between British English and American English.

Japanese students typically do not ask questions of their teachers, but the students he had were different. They were either students at elite universities, such as the University of Tokyo, Keio University, or Hosei University, or they were senior practitioners of Kodokan Judo (講道館柔道). These elite students must have asked many questions, as did the judo practitioners with Kano's encouragement. The intention of these *judoka* was not to become karate experts but to introduce some of the karate techniques into judo, if possible, or to find a way to fight against the *karateka*.

It can easily be assumed that these university students asked him why Original Shodan was so much more difficult and why they had to start with this *kata*. I can't imagine the insurmountable task of trying to explain the deep meaning of the true intentions of his sensei, Itosu, especially in light of the significant language barrier.

Therefore, I suspect that Funakoshi decided to switch the order these two *kata* just as he changed the reading of the characters from *Pin'an* to *Heian*.

Mystery 3: The First Step

Why is the first step of the Heian *kata* always to the left side? When you are in a fight, isn't it more natural and advantageous to position your opponent in front of you? So, why do we not teach beginners to move forward or backward with techniques pointing toward the front? Are we learning to fight an opponent who stands off to our left side? Do you not wonder why? Is there a specific meaning to this? Was it maybe a fluke or unintentional?

It is interesting to realize that, before the Pin'an (Heian) series was created toward the end of the nineteenth century, the first *kata* for Shuri Te, the forefather of Shotokan, was Naihanchi (Tekki). The uniqueness of Tekki is that this *kata* uses only *kiba dachi*. It is also interesting that all three Tekki *kata* start to the right side and that the initial techniques are executed to the right.

Let's look at the other eight major JKA *kata* and check the direction of both the starting movement and the initial technique.

- Bassai Dai: step forward and execute the first technique toward the front.
- Kanku Dai: shift the left foot into *kokutsu dachi* toward the left side and execute the first technique to the left side.
- Jion: step backward and execute the first technique toward the front.
- Jutte (Jitte): step backward and execute the first technique toward the front.
- Enpi: shift the left foot to a kneeling position toward the left side and execute the first tech-

nique toward the front.

- Gankaku: step backward and execute the first technique toward the front.
- Hangetsu: step forward and execute the first technique toward the front.
- Meikyo: shift the right foot into *kiba dachi* and execute the first technique toward the front.

The tally is two *kata* that step forward, three that step backward, two that step to the left, and one that steps to the right. It is interesting that only one of these eight major *kata*, Meikyo, starts to the right side. So, it looks as though stepping to the left is very popular, but we need to examine this more closely.

In Kanku Dai, the first step and the initial technique are done to the left. However, in Enpi and Meikyo (明鏡), the techniques are executed to the front even though the foot movement is to the side. Given these statistics, let's think about why the ancient Okinawan masters picked Tekki *kata*, which starts to the right side and uses only *kiba dachi*. This is a very interesting topic, but we will not go too deeply into this as we are trying to figure out why all Heian *kata* start to the left.

Whether you go to the left or right, one thing is clear: Itosu did not make the first move go forward or backward. He chose to go sideways in all five Heian *kata*. Why? The hint is Tekki as it also starts sideways. I believe this was clearly intentional and that the Okinawan masters' deep understanding of kinesiology is evidenced here.

Let's look at three directions and evaluate why he chose sideways. It is pretty easy to figure out why he did not pick a backward step. He obviously did not want to teach beginners to retreat. It is, of course, best to move forward. OK, then why didn't he pick a forward step?

Take a look at the shape of the foot. We all know it is long in length and narrow in width. By examining the bone structure, we see that the shinbone, or tibia, is placed not in the center but rather close to the heel. Our walking ability seems so natural that we do not think about how we walk, but the mechanism of bipedalism is a truly complex and precise one.

The front part of our foot is purposely longer because it is designed to make it easier for us to stay standing upright. This is why it is easier to fall backward than forward. You can experiment with this easily by feeling the difference between your forward balance and your backward balance. Indeed, stepping forward takes some effort. This is exactly why short-distance runners have a gadget to raise their heels high and why they need to lean forward so much to start quickly.

I am sure you agree that a quick start is critical to a hundred-meter sprint when you are racing to win or lose by a difference of a hundredth of a second. Believe it or not, this quick start is just as critical, if not more so, in karate. Wouldn't you think so if you were fighting for your life? However, in a karate fight, we do not have a gadget to raise our heels, nor can we lean forward as much as in a hundred-meter sprint.

In Chapter 9: "Unstable Balance," I use an analogy with the Leaning Tower of Pisa to explain the special mechanism in the initial movements of Bassai Dai. That mechanism in Bassai Dai is there to teach practitioners how to shift forward quickly. This is a highly technical movement; therefore, the ancient masters chose to make the first move to the side in the beginner's *kata*, which are Tekki and Heian.

You can experiment with this to check which way is faster: stepping toward the front or stepping to the left. If you lean sideways, you will realize that there is little support or resistance from the leg muscles to slow your movement. You can feel that the Achilles tendon does not stop your fall to the side. Besides, taking a stance, especially *neko ashi dachi* (eventually *kokutsu dachi*), to the side is anatomically easier than taking it toward the front. As we are so used to stepping toward the front in our normal life activities, we feel strange if we have to step to the side. However, you can learn how to shift smoothly by repeating this side-shifting movement.

This quick-shifting ability is one of the most important study points of the Tekki *kata*. The ancient masters are telling us through Tekki, "If you have no unnecessary resistance in the initial move, you can shift to the side very quickly." Once we learn how to do this to the side, we can translate the technique to forward movement, and the first *kata* after Tekki is Bassai Dai, which teaches us how to shift forward quickly. This learning method is so excellent that when I discovered this fact, I was honestly shocked by the depth of the ancient masters' physiological understanding.

Some devil's advocates may say, "OK, I agree that shifting sideways is fast, but shifting backward is also easier and faster than going forward." This is true, and the first step of some *kata*, such as Jion, Jutte (十手), and Gankaku, is backward.

In Chapter 5: "Disparity between Kata and Kumite," I discuss why moving backward is a bad choice in a fight, which is the major reason I am against *sanbon kumite* and *gohon kumite* for intermediate and advanced students. The ancient masters knew this, of course, so they did not emphasize the backward step and did not pick it for the initial *kata*. When we better understand the mechanics involved, we do not step back in Jion, Jutte, and Gankaku. In fact, we sink down in position with one foot stepping back more or less for support.

So, Itosu understood the importance of Tekki as the initial *kata* for karate beginners; however, it can be extremely difficult to perform correctly, particularly with regard to the arm techniques. Thus, he decided that it was not appropriate for children in the public school physical education program and that a different type of *kata* was needed. This is why an introductory *kata*, Pin'an, was created and introduced into the public school system in the early twentieth century. As all the Naihanchi *kata* started to the right side, Itosu chose to start all the Pin'an *kata* to the left to create balance.

Whichever Heian *kata* you perform, your left foot must not pivot as you take your first step. What must happen first is the shifting of your hip joints so that the hip or midsection of your body will be pushed slightly to the left while the up-

per body is erect and the feet remain unmoved in *shizentai* (自然体, 'natural stance'). This has the effect of putting you into an unbalanced state of balance, the details of which are covered in Chapter 9. Before too much body weight falls onto the left leg, you must take a quick step to your left.

It is interesting to note that the first stance of Current Shodan is *zenkutsu dachi*, while for the other Heian *kata* (Current Nidan through Heian Godan), the first stance is *kokutsu dachi*. I believe this was also intentional on the part of Itosu. In the original Pin'an *kata*, they did not have *kokutsu dachi*; it was all *neko ashi dachi*. He wanted to put a more challenging stance, *zenkutsu dachi*, in the simplest *kata*, Current Shodan, since *neko ashi dachi* is short and is made more readily.

Now that you understand the purpose of the first steps in the Heian and Tekki *kata*, I hope you will appreciate and enjoy them more when you perform them.

押忍

CHAPTER THREE
第三章

HEIAN BUNKAI MYSTERIES
平安形分解の謎

Believe it or not, when I learned Heian *kata* for the first time in Japan some fifty years ago, the *bunkai* (分解) were never taught to us in class. When I started to teach and visit different dojo in the U.S. in the seventies, I found that a lot of strange *bunkai* were being taught in many dojo. By "strange," I mean the *bunkai* were unrealistic and almost unusable.

Of course, there are different levels of *bunkai* for a given technique; therefore, I admit that there can be many different interpretations. In short, if a technique works, then we can say that it is an acceptable *bunkai*. However, some widely accepted interpretations are not realistic, and I feel strongly that better interpretations should be taught; thus, that is exactly what I wish to do here. I will point out some unrealistic *bunkai* from the Heian series and then offer a better interpretation for each one.

1.   Three Successive Rising Blocks in Shodan

There is a sequence of three *jodan age uke* (上段上げ受け) in Heian Shodan. In my previous book, *Shotokan Myths*, I talked about the strange *bunkai* shown in a well-known organization's videotape. In this video, the attacker attacks with *mae geri* followed by a *jodan* punch. The defender blocks with *gedan*

barai (下段払い) and *jodan kaishu age uke* (上段開手上げ受け). This part is fine, but what is strange is the following two steps.

The attacker actually steps back to throw the second and the third punches as the defender steps forward to block with *jodan age uke*. Do you not think it strange that someone would step back to throw a punch, especially twice in a row? Then, the last *jodan age uke* is interpreted as an attack to the joint of the opponent's *jodan oi zuki* arm. This is doable as an interpretation, but it's not realistic as the joint attack is done slowly, and then the attacker is released.

First, let's figure out why *jodan age uke* was performed three times in a row. Before I get into the actual interpretations, I must explain one other thing about the names of the techniques. Unbelievable as it may sound to most Western readers, these names were invented only a hundred years ago, when karate was introduced into the public schools. Until that time, the teacher would only show the technique and say, "This technique is done this way, that way, etc." Therefore, there was no relationship between the name *jodan age uke* and the technique that we understand that to be today.

I hope I am not confusing the reader, but this is a very important point that must be understood. Let me explain why it is important. If you hear the term *jodan age uke*, you have an idea of how it is done and what it is for. This is exactly what the Okinawan masters did not want because this particular movement can be other techniques rather than just a fixed *jodan age uke*.

This means there are several different interpretations that are possible for this simple *jodan age uke* technique. So, it is not three instances of *jodan age uke* as the attacker steps back. We need to learn at least three different uses of this technique.

In Heian Shodan, these are, in fact, three different counterattacks. The only *jodan age uke* would be the very first one, which is performed in the sixth step, right after the *gedan barai*. Even though you step forward three times, the correct interpretation is to have three *jodan* counterattack options.

The first option is a rising hammer fist to the opponent's neck or chin. The second option is a hook punch to the side of the opponent's head. The third option could be a *jodan nobashi zuki* (上段伸ばし突き)—a punch that comes from the center of the body rather than from the hip—to the opponent's chin.

All three applications are executed based on the concept that, within the first move, the front open hand blocks the *jodan* attack and grabs the wrist, which is followed by a step forward with a counterattack. If you are not familiar with or have not used these applications in *ippon kumite* training, I suggest you include them in the *kumite* syllabus as they are very usable and effective.

2. First Technique in Nidan

This move is said to be a *jodan uchi uke* (上段内受け) with the front arm and a *jodan kamae* (上段構え) with the rear arm. I explained earlier that the names really do not describe the actual techniques themselves. However, many practitioners and instructors have mistakenly been led to believe they are exactly what the names say they are.

If you believe the purpose of the rear arm is only *jodan kamae*, then you have underestimated the effectiveness of karate techniques. This is definitely not just an extra level of protection for the face. The better interpretation is that this rear arm is executing *jodan uke*.

So, what is the front arm, then? This is, in fact, a *jodan* uppercut to the opponent's chin. The fist is turned to look like an *uke*, but the original move was to set the front hand in an uppercut position (with the palm facing the defender). You can see proof of this if you study Shito Ryu's Pin'an. They kept the original hand position with the front fist executing *jodan age zuki* (上段上げ突き). Yes, the front hand is not for blocking but for punching the opponent.

This first move is a very technically challenging move, but it's a true karate move in which a block and a counter are performed simultaneously. Doesn't that make more sense?

3. Second Technique in Nidan

In the same *bunkai* video, the defender is expected to catch a *chudan* punch with this technique. Please try this with an opponent and experience how unrealistic this interpretation is.

The better, or more realistic, interpretation is a simultaneous block-and-attack technique just like the one we saw for the very first move. For this second technique, the front hand executes *jodan soto uke* (上段外受け) or *nagashi uke,* and the rear hand simultaneously executes a *chudan ura zuki* (中段裏突き).

Executing a block and a counterattack simultaneously is the most effective and efficient method. Wouldn't you favor this concept over the "unique" and circuslike technique of catching a punch with both forearms?

4. *Kosa Uke* in Sandan

This is an interesting technique, and I clearly remember having tremendous difficulty in executing it correctly when I first learned this *kata* even though it was so many years ago. The technique is said to be a simultaneous *gedan barai* and *chudan uchi uke* (中段内受け). Some practitioners call this *kosa uke* (交叉受け); however, I do not agree with this term.

Kosa (交叉) means 'cross', and, viewing these techniques from the side, it may look like a cross (photo left), but the arms are, in fact, not crossed. The *gedan* and *jodan* crossed-arm blocks we see in Heian Godan are real *kosa uke,* though I do not believe the true *bunkai* for those consists of blocks, but I will cover this later in this chapter. So, I contend that this is not a multiblock technique.

It is possible, though uncommon, for an attacker to throw a *morote chudan zuki* (諸手中段突き). It is more realistic to believe that the attacker extends his arms to

grab the defender's lapel. But, even if you believe that one of these attacks is fea-
sible—either the double-fisted attack or the lapel grab—it is unrealistic and even
humorous to expect to block both arms with one *chudan uke* and one *gedan barai*.
If you do not believe this, I suggest you try it with a partner at your dojo.

Again, the problem has arisen because of the name of the technique. The name
is *uke*, but this is not a combination of two blocks. The mystery disappears when
you remember that the key to this karate technique is a combination of a block and
a simultaneous counterattack.

The *bunkai* goes like this: After the first *chudan uchi uke* (with the left arm),
your left wrist is grabbed by the opponent. The explanation for the supposed *kosa
uke* is that you first twist the left arm inward and then bring the right forearm from
the outside, rotating it back toward you to break the wrist grab. Right after the grab
is broken, you counterattack with a right *jodan uraken uchi* (上段裏拳打ち). This
is why the stance is *heisoku dachi* (閉足立ち, 'closed-foot stance'), which can be,
in actual application, either *heiko dachi* (平行立ち, 'parallel stance') or *sanchin
dachi* (サンチン立ち, '*sanchin* stance').

5. First Technique in Yondan

I have already explained the first move in
Nidan. The first move in Yondan is similar but
uses a *kaishu* (開手, 'open hand') instead of a
fist, so I am sure the reader will immediately
guess the correct *bunkai*. Yes, the rear arm is
a *jodan* block, and the front *shuto* is used to
spear the neck or eyes.

I need to emphasize here that I am not dis-
counting the popular interpretation of using
the front arm as a *jodan uke*. It is doable to first block and then throw a counterattack with the rear *shuto*, though this is not included in this particular move. The

timing of such a *bunkai* would be broken into two consecutive movements, which is slow. The *bunkai* I am presenting here is simultaneous (a block and a counterattack at the same time), which is a more effective technique. The mystery is solved when we realize that these two arm movements are a simultaneous block-and-counter technique.

However, I wondered why the first two moves (*kokutsu dachi* to the left and right sides) were done slowly. I wondered if there was any meaning to this. When you review the Shito Ryu and Shorin Ryu versions of Pin'an Yondan, you find that these two moves are done fast or at a normal speed just like the first moves in Nidan.

Interestingly, they are also done at a fast speed in Wado Ryu, which branched off from Shotokan in the early thirties. So, Funakoshi taught the first two moves at a normal speed in the twenties then, somewhere in the mid or late thirties, decided to slow these movements down. As far as I know, there is no written document explaining why he changed the speed, so we can only guess.

I tried to imagine him teaching this *kata* to hundreds of university students. Funakoshi's favorite *kata* was Kosokun (Kanku Dai), and, interestingly, the first two moves are identical in these two *kata*. In the original *kata*, Kosokun, the stance for these two moves was *neko ashi dachi*. After he changed the stance to *kokutsu dachi*, he might have felt the difficulty of executing these two techniques at high speed.

As a conscious educator, he might have decided to slow these two moves down in Yondan. By doing this, the students would learn to coordinate the leg movement (getting into *kokutsu dachi*) and the arm technique. He might have hoped the students would learn these first two moves of Heian Yondan better by doing them slowly. He probably believed that the students would do Kanku Dai better once they reached *shodan* level. Again, this is just speculation on my part, and there is no proof that he felt this way.

6. *Yoko Geri Keage/Jodan Uraken Uchi* Combination in Nidan and Yondan

This combination is found in both Heian Nidan and Heian Yondan. In fact, it is
done the same way in other *kata*, as well,
such as Kanku Dai and Gankaku.

First of all, I need to explain why I've
brought up this combination. Frankly, for
many years, I could not understand the
purpose of the *uraken uchi* that is executed
simultaneously with the kick. We were encouraged to kick high, which made me
wonder where I was supposed to be attacking with my *uraken uchi*. If the kick is
to the midsection, and if the opponent is bent over, then I could possibly see my
uraken uchi hitting the opponent. However, there are two points that puzzled me.

One point was the obvious shortness of my arm. When you kick an opponent
with a *yoko geri keage*, it is impossible to reach him with your *uraken uchi*. The
second point was regarding why it must be done simultaneously. It was a mystery
for a long time as *bunkai* was never fully explained to me.

First, I thought maybe the punch was a follow-up technique after the kick, but
we were told to execute these two techniques at the same time. So, I investigated
by reviewing the Pin'an *kata* of Shito Ryu and Shorin Ryu. By reviewing those
kata, I noticed that they did not have *yoko geri keage*. Instead, the kicks in the original versions of what are now Heian Nidan and Heian Yondan were all *mae geri*.

Funakoshi introduced several new techniques after his immigration to Tokyo,
and *yoko geri keage* was one of them. Chapter 1 covers the subject of why Funakoshi introduced techniques that were not found on Okinawa. It is a very interesting
subject from the perspective of Shotokan karate history, and there we find many
facts that are not well known. We will not go into why he made these changes in
this chapter, but I will cover the disparity that arose from the changes he made.

In Shito Ryu's Pin'an Shodan (Shotokan's Heian Nidan), we find that the technique is a *chudan uchi ude uke* (中段内腕受け) with a *chudan mae geri* (中段

前蹴り). If you have a chance, I suggest you go to *YouTube* and examine it for yourself. If you look closely, you will find that the block is done before the kick, and this timing makes sense when you consider its *bunkai*. You block first and then quickly counterattack with a *chudan mae geri*.

Interestingly, in Yondan, the arm is straight and looks like a *chudan kentsui uchi* (中段拳槌打ち). This technique makes sense as I assume it was originally a *gedan barai* before the *mae geri*. As the switch to the higher kicks of modern-day karate became popular, it was natural that the blocking arm would be placed higher, as well.

When Funakoshi changed the kick to *yoko geri keage*, he had to change the arm technique accordingly. The reason is quite obvious. Try to do a *yoko uchi uke* (横内受け) with a *yoko geri keage*. You will find it almost impossible to execute this combination. With a side kick, an extended arm is much easier and works much better.

So, why did he replace the *gedan barai* or *kentsui uchi* with an *uraken uchi*, then? The puzzle continued. It's actually easier to execute *kentsui uchi* than *uraken uchi* with *yoko geri keage*, but he chose the *uraken uchi*. I concluded that Funakoshi chose the *uraken uchi* because it uses a snapping motion, which works better with a snap kick.

Unfortunately, the *bunkai* concept went out the window with *yoko geri keage* and *uraken uchi* being used for all *kata*. In the popular *bunkai* video, the *uraken uchi* is used to block a *chudan zuki*. They got the right idea, but the performer misses both punches. However, it is done so quickly that no one probably noticed this error. To do this technique correctly, all they had to do was a *gedan barai* before the *yoko geri keage*.

Another option is, of course, to follow the method in the video and try to block the *chudan zuki* with the *uraken uchi*. This is difficult to do, but it can be done. With a *yoko geri keage*, I believe the best interpretation would be a *chudan tsukami uke* (中段掴み受け) followed by a *yoko geri keage*. First, you block the *chudan zuki* with a *gedan barai*. Then, you grab the opponent's wrist and pull your arm in as you execute a *yoko geri keage* to the opponent's armpit or chin. I suggest that the reader try all these different options to see which one is workable and realistic.

7. *Kagi Zuki* in Godan

I am not an expert in judo, but I took four years of it and attained the rank of *shodan* before switching to karate when I was in high school. When my sensei asked if I could figure out a *bunkai* for the *kagi zuki* (鉤突き) in Heian Godan, I knew it was a throw. I had practiced doing this throw called *uki goshi* (浮腰, 'floating hip') thousands of times.

Take a look at the illustration to the right and notice that the guy doing the throw is in *heisoku dachi*. Notice that this technique is done slowly, unlike the *kagi zuki* in Tekki, which is done quickly and powerfully. So, this

Uki-goshi

is an indication that this technique is not a *kagi zuki* even though the final position looks like it. It is a more slowly moving technique, a throwing technique.

In the same *bunkai* video from before, this is interpreted as a joint attack to the elbow, and I consider this to be a good option. However, you will notice that the first instance of this technique (the third move in the *kata*) is completely ignored. If they had included the *uki goshi* in the *bunkai*, it would have been more beneficial to the audience. Take a look at the interesting photo to the left of Funakoshi doing the *bunkai*. What do you think of this?

8. *Kosa Uke* or *Juji Uke* in Godan

Gedan kosa uke (下段交叉受け), or juji uke (十字
受け), is typically taught as a pressing block to *mae geri*.
Yes, this is possible if the kicker is extremely slow. You
might say, "I can do it with the attacker kicking at full
speed." OK, maybe so in *ippon kumite*, but would you use
this in *jiyu kumite*? I am not saying this *bunkai* is wrong.
If it works, then it is a good *bunkai*. I am only saying there
is a better interpretation, which is not popular.

The inside (or bottom) arm is a block, either a *gedan
barai* or an *osae uke* to a *chudan zuki*, and the upper arm
is actually used as a *gedan* or *chudan zuki*. As I have mentioned before, the original idea of karate techniques was
to block and counter in one move.

Juji-Uke

Then, how about the second *kosa uke*, which is an open-handed version? A
popular *bunkai* is to interpret this as a *jodan* block using both hands. Now, what
you have to remember here is that the attacker executed a *mae geri* first, and this
was supposedly blocked by a *gedan kosa uke*. Try this combination with a dojo
colleague. The attacker's *jodan* punch has to be very slow, or he has to allow a long
pause before punching in order for your *jodan* block to be able to catch the punch.
In other words, this is not a realistic technique. Besides, why would you use both
hands to block a *jodan* punch and leave your midsection completely exposed? This
cannot be a very wise move.

So, let's go back to the original concept of the
Okinawan karate *bunkai*, which was a block and a
counterattack thrown at the same time. Once you
understand this, it is very easy to figure this out.
The top hand (the right hand in the photo to the
left) executes an open-handed *jodan age uke*, and
the bottom hand (the left hand in the same photo)
executes a *shuto uchi* to the attacker's throat. An-

other, more aggressive, interpretation is to throw a *shuto kosa uchi* (手刀交叉打ち) to the neck. In other words, using both *shuto*, you strike upward toward the opponent's neck in a scissor form. This technique will strike the jugular veins on both sides of the neck and can be a very dangerous attack, but I think this is what the ancient Okinawan masters had in mind for this *bunkai*.

9.   Jump in Godan

Here is another commonly mis-interpreted technique. Just like the photo shown here, you are to jump over a stick that has been aimed at your legs. The previously men-tioned *bunkai* video shows the same concept. But, ask yourself where you would attack if you had a stick like this. Is attacking the legs your first choice? If I had a stick, I would strike the guy on the head or the torso. Unless you are a superman, you cannot jump over such a strike.

You may say, "But, this is a jump, and our teacher told us to jump as high as we could." This is another misinterpretation of a karate technique, similar to the case of the mismatch between the name of the technique and its actual application. We find many jumps in *kata*, and many of them are indeed jumps, such as those per-formed with kicks in Kanku Dai and Gankaku or with an elbow strike in Meikyo. However, some are throws. Then, why did the *kata* creator pick a jump to "hide" a throw? It is an easy guess. He wanted to include some leg exercises to strengthen the legs, not hide the throw.

The *bunkai* for the jump in Enpi is also a throw, but let's get back to this tech-nique in Godan. The technique right before the jump is an uppercut to the chin, and this is perfect as you grab the opponent's lapel with the punching hand, grab his

sleeve with the other hand, and then throw him.

Remember the *uki goshi* as the interpretation of the *kagi zuki* from before? This throw, which is called *morote seoi nage* (諸手背負い投げ) and is shown in the photo to the left, is another popular throw in judo.

A throw makes more sense when you realize that the technique that comes right after the jump is to land in *kosa dachi* while executing *gedan kosa uke*. If you prefer to interpret the jump as a jump over a stick, then how do you interpret the technique that follows it? Some have told me, "The person who attacked with the staff throws a *mae geri*, so I block with a crossed-arm block." I have to call this another circus act. I am sorry, but everybody knows this is not realistic.

If you interpret this jump as a throw, then the mystery disappears. After you throw the opponent, and if you do not let go of the lapel and the sleeve you are holding onto, your arms can cross as in the photo to the right.

Or, you can add the interpretation that, after the throw, you finish the opponent off with a punch to the face. You may not like the idea of punching a person on the ground, but according to karate concepts, it makes perfect sense to finish the opponent with a punch after a throw.

Here again, I suggest that the reader try this *bunkai* to see if it makes more sense. You need to be very careful how you throw your karate colleague unless he is familiar with judo falls. You could hurt your colleague badly if you throw him right onto the hard floor. I suggest you use the rubberized mats that are used for wrestling or gymnastics to prevent any possible injury.

10. *Manji Uke* in Godan

This *uke* is popular as we find it in many other *kata*, such as Jion, Jutte, and Gankaku. The front arm is easy as this is a *gedan uke*, which we know well. The mystery is the rear arm. This is a *jodan uchi uke*, so the most popular *bunkai* is to block a *jodan* punch.

The worst interpretation I have seen is the double block against two attackers, one in front and one behind. Again, I have to call this a circus act if it is done while you are looking forward. Do you have eyes in the back of your head? How can you block a punch that is coming from behind you? You may say, "I look back when I block the punch." This is exactly how it is shown in the popular *bunkai* video, but then the performer lets the attacker go without any counterattack. Is this realistic?

This video does a great job on the *bunkai* for the two *manji uke* (卍受け) except for this small action. Before the *manji uke*, you cross the arms—this is interpreted as a simultaneous *jodan nagashi uke* and *gedan* open-handed strike—and then throw the opponent. I believe this is a very appropriate *bunkai*. The rear arm is held high not to execute a *jodan uke* but to emphasize that this arm has to be pulled strongly and thrust upward in order to throw the opponent. In other words, this high rear arm is a form that has been exaggerated for *kata*.

However, if you feel that you need to see another option besides throwing, the following can be considered. The first move is the same; the upper hand is a *jodan nagashi uke*, and the lower hand is a *gedan* open-handed attack. But, the attacker then throws a second *jodan* punch. Your *gedan* hand comes up and throws the *jodan nagashi uke* as the other hand throws either a *chudan* or a *gedan* punch.

I have found it extremely difficult to describe these *bunkai* moves in English due to my lack of language skills. I hope the reader at least got the general idea and will try these interpretations to see if they make sense. Again, there can be many levels of interpretation to a given technique, so my interpretations are certainly not the only ones that are correct or realistic.

If you are interested in *bunkai*, there is an excellent book called *Hidden Karate* (隠されていた空手 [Champ, 2006]), written by Gennosuke Higaki (桧垣 源之助), which has been translated into English. My interpretations are somewhat different from his, but the basic concepts I learned from my sensei coincide with what he presents in this book.

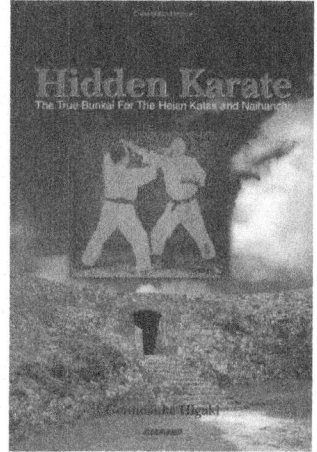

I want to conclude this chapter with a few more comments. As I said before, *kata* is only a model with various popular techniques. We must know the *bunkai*, but there are many different kinds and depths of interpretation. All are good if they work not only in the dojo but also in a real-life situation. We must not be trapped in a fixed notion of a particular *bunkai*. We must not spend our time on "circus" techniques. Most karate techniques are simple and direct. I hope more Shotokan practitioners will spend time studying *bunkai* so as to understand *kata* better, which will lead to a better appreciation of this treasure that was handed down to us over hundreds of years.

CHAPTER FOUR
第四章

MIKAZUKI GERI, AN EXTINCT KICK?
三日月蹴りの謎

We know that *mikazuki geri* (三日月蹴り) means 'crescent kick'. You will be familiar with this kick if you are an advanced student as it is found not only in Heian Godan and Bassai Dai but also in Meikyo and Hangetsu (半月). So, you could say this is a popular kick in our *kata*. In fact, it is the third-most popular kick in Shotokan *kata* after *mae geri* and *yoko geri keage*. OK, now you will probably ask, "So, what is the problem?" There is no problem at all, but I have had a nagging question, and I want to share it here.

Here is the question: how often do you practice this kick in *kihon* training at your dojo? If your answer is "many times" or "often," then your *kihon* program is very comprehensive and your training is well rounded. But, most readers will probably have to confess that their answer is "not often" or even "never." Truthfully, what is it like at your dojo?

My next question is this: do you know the reason or reasons that it is not included in your organization's *kyu* syllabus? Go ask your sensei, but I doubt he will be able to give you a satisfactory answer. Please do not read this chapter and then test your sensei by asking this question. You have to promise not to do this before reading on.

At most dojo, the first kick a white belt learns is *mae geri* ('front kick'). As soon as he gets promoted to eighth *kyu*, he learns other kicks, such as *yoko geri keage* ('side snap kick'), *yoko geri kekomi* ('side thrust kick'), and *mawashi geri* ('roundhouse kick' or 'round kick'). He is expected to practice all these kicks in his regular *kihon* training. However, he will most likely not learn *mikazuki geri* or *ushiro geri* (後ろ蹴り, 'rear kick' or 'back kick').

We can probably agree that *ushiro geri* is too difficult for a blue belt, but I have always wondered why *mikazuki geri* is not taught. Have you ever wondered why we practice *mawashi geri* often, yet *mikazuki geri*, a kick similar to *mawashi geri*, is not included in the regular *kihon* program?

Unfortunately, I do not have access to the exam syllabi of all Shotokan organizations, but by reviewing those of the JKA and the JKS, to which I happen to have access, we find that this particular kick is not included in the *kihon* requirements. It's no wonder *mikazuki geri* is not included in the regular dojo training of these two major organizations.

To support this point, let's look at the "Bible" of the JKA, *Dynamic Karate* (Kodansha, 1966 [photo right]), authored by Masatoshi Nakayama (中山正敏, 1913–1987), and find out how much space is given to *mikazuki geri* compared to *mawashi geri*. As suspected, *mikazuki geri* receives only half a page (p. 158), whereas *mawashi geri* enjoys three full pages (pp. 155–157). Obviously, the author considered *mawashi geri* to be much more important than *mikazuki geri* as inferred from the space allotted to each kick.

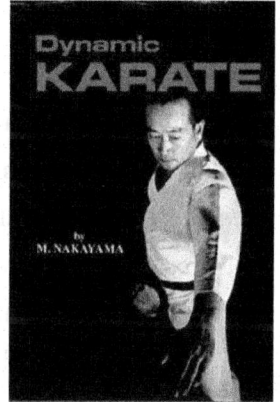

For your information, *yoko geri* receives five pages (pp. 150–154), and even *ushiro geri* gets two full pages (pp. 159–160). The only other kick that receives just half a page is *gyaku mawashi geri* ('reverse roundhouse kick'), which shares page 158 with *mikazuki geri*. So, you can easily guess the importance that Nakayama ascribed to *mikazuki geri*.

Let me quote what he says about this kick in *Dynamic Karate*:

Mikazuki Geri (Crescent Kick)

When an opponent attempts to attack with a punch, block his forearm as he steps close and counterattack with the crescent kick to his abdomen or groin. In this instance, kick with the ball of the foot. The crescent kick is sometimes used as a block. For example, when the opponent attempts a punch to your body, kick his forearm to the side as he attacks. Use the sole of the foot to apply the block.

Important points:

The course the kicking foot travels is shorter in the crescent kick than in the round kick. Another difference is that in the crescent kick it is unnecessary to raise the leg to the side before kicking. The kick can be delivered directly from the original position on the ground. It follows, then, that compared with the round kick, the crescent kick is less powerful, but lends itself better to a surprise attack.

As you can see, the amount of explanation given for *mikazuki geri* in this book is unfortunately very small. In addition, only *gedan* and *chudan* applications are mentioned; *jodan* is omitted. I do not know why the author did not include any *jodan* applications. Just like *mawashi geri*, this kick is most effective when it is delivered to the face level as its line of travel is horizontal at the time of impact.

Now we must compare these two kicks more clearly and identify the differences. We need to check to see if there is any relationship between these two kicks or if they are two totally different kicks. Hopefully, we will be able to discover the apparent reasons for which *mawashi geri* is commonly practiced but *mikazuki geri* is not.

Mawashi Geri (回し蹴り)

Let us look at the mechanics of *mawashi geri*, which we practice often in our *kihon*. First, you get into a good *zenkutsu dachi*. Then, you shift your weight to the front leg (supporting leg) as you need to lift the rear leg (kicking leg) up.

Your instructor will give you a very interesting instruction next. He will say, "Lift your foot behind you." So, this means you will be standing in a one-legged position with your rear foot up in the air but tucked behind you. Then, he will tell you to rotate your hips and the knee of your kicking leg horizontally. The teacher will also tell you to rotate your supporting foot outward so that you can get full hip rotation (see the illustration above). He may also encourage you to swing your arms in the direction opposite that of your hip and leg rotation to add extra twisting power to your kick.

So, if you listen to your instructor, and if you execute this kick exactly how he tells you to, then boom! You will have a very powerful kick. If you try this kick on a large sandbag, it makes a great sound. Bang! Yes, it sounds very powerful.

Well, in execution, we may not be able to bring our foot to the rear as the instructor demands, but we try like heck to lift the knee of our kicking leg high so the tucked leg will be in a horizontal position. We practice this hundreds or maybe thousands of times. Tournament competitors love to practice this kick as it is a useful kick in *shiai*. Indeed, after *mae geri*, *mawashi geri* is the second-most popular kick for scoring points.

World-renowned Masahiko Tana-ka (田中昌彦, 1941– [photo right]) had a *mawashi geri* that was very impressive, and he won the world championship several times with his signature kick in the seventies. His *kirikaeshi mawashi geri* (切り返し回し蹴り, 'hip-switching roundhouse kick') was so fast and beautiful. Yes, this was some thirty years ago, so many of our younger readers may not have seen his technique, but I believe some instructional clips are available on *YouTube*.

Mikazuki Geri (三日月蹴り)

Now, let us look at the mechanics of *mikazuki geri*. Notice that we execute this kick from a *kiba dachi* in Heian Godan, Bassai, and Meikyo. In Hangetsu, we do this kick from a *kokutsu dachi*. Isn't it interesting that it is not executed from a *zenkutsu dachi*? So what does this mean? There is definitely a reason behind it, and I will share my thoughts on this later.

Let us continue to look at the mechanics of this kick. Another unique point or requirement for this kick in all *kata* is that you must set your front hand. This hand becomes a stationary target, and you are expected to kick it, which is supposed to make a good slapping sound. This is unique as we do not do this for any of the *mae geri* or *yoko geri* in *kata*. Do you not wonder why? We will discuss the possible reasons for this particular requirement in the section below.

Why are only *kiba dachi* and *kokutsu dachi* used?

What do these two stances have in common? Both of them are straight stances that hide the groin area.

On Okinawa, they discouraged all kicks to start out. There are several reasons for discouraging kicks. One of them is obviously the poor balance that comes from standing on one leg. The other is that the speed of a kick is much slower than that of a hand technique. Lastly, but most importantly as it pertains to the present subject, kicks tend to expose the groin area, and this was considered to be undesirable in a *kumite* situation. This is why the only kick that was recommended or even found in the original *kata* was *mae geri*, which was aimed only at the *gedan*, never at the *jodan*.

When Funakoshi Sensei learned Shuri Te *kata* on Okinawa, most of the *kata* he learned did not have *yoko geri*. For instance, the *yoko geri* of Heian Nidan and Heian Yondan were *mae geri*. Take a look at the Pin'an forms of Shito Ryu and Shorin Ryu of Okinawa. They still do these *kata* with *mae geri*. So, it makes sense to deliver *mikazuki geri* from these straight stances. When delivering a kick from either of these two stances, the groin area will have minimal exposure.

Another more refined reason that these two stances are chosen for *mikazuki geri* is their hip position. *Mikazuki geri* requires extra hip rotation at the end of the kick, and these stances allow for more of that rotation than *zenkutsu dachi*.

Why must the kick hit an extended hand?

There are at least two good reasons for this. The first is that the extended arm with the target hand signifies that you need to grab the opponent's sleeve or clothes in order to (A) assist you with your balance as you initiate the kick and (B) pull or yank the opponent toward you to get maximum impact when you land the kick.

The second reason is that *mikazuki geri* is a type of *kekomi geri* ('thrusting kick') in which the foot travels in a circular motion, and the impact must be delivered horizontally (aimed at the solar plexus or head). This is a different kind of *kekomi geri* from *yoko kekomi geri*, where the leg is extended fully in the direction of the kick. It is extremely difficult to stop *mikazuki geri* in midair because of the way this kick is executed. Try and see if you can stop a *mikazuki geri* without hitting your hand. Yes, it can be done, but I am sure you found it difficult. Well, I have actually seen some students miss their hand while executing this kick and literally lose their balance. So, now you know that this hand-slapping action is needed to stop this kick in midair.

So, the points I listed above are the practical reasons for the unique requirements of *mikazuki geri*. Now you may be wondering if we can execute *mikazuki geri* from our most popular stance, *zenkutsu dachi*. Of course we can. You raise the kicking leg as though you were going to execute *mae geri*. Then, at the halfway point—to be more accurate, I should say, "somewhere in the middle"—you rotate your hips and change the direction of the kick from vertical to horizontal.

This is obviously more challenging than executing this same kick from a *kiba dachi* because *zenkutsu dachi* does not allow for as great an angle for the hip rotation, but it is possible. Besides, from a *zenkutsu dachi*, one can easily execute a *mae geri*, and that would be the most effective kicking technique.

What are the differences between these two kicks?

First of all, *mikazuki geri* does not require the knee to be tucked up. The kicking leg is kept fairly straight and swung without a snap. This technique is similar to that of *furiken uchi* (振り拳打ち, 'swinging-fist strike'), which was a favorite technique of the late Asai Sensei.

Secondly, the whole foot, instead of just a part (e.g., the ball or the heel), will land on the target. The kicking foot is typically pointed vertically in *mikazuki geri*, whereas it is normally horizontal in *mawashi geri*, regardless of whether the ball or the instep of the foot is used.

Thirdly, the hip movements are completely different. In *mikazuki geri*, the initial hip movement is closer to that of *mae geri* than that of *mawashi geri*. In other words, the pelvis is tucked up instead of being rotated around. Then, the whole leg is raised up, and, about midway through, the hip executes a small but quick horizontal whipping action, which brings the leg inward (i.e., toward the target). Even at the moment of contact, the hip is still facing forward as in *mae geri*. The power of the kick comes from the whipping of the leg at the last moment, similar to *furiken uchi*.

Let's look at *mawashi geri*. We practice this kick more frequently; thus, I assume the reader is more familiar with the kinesiological mechanics of this kick. The biggest difference is that the first movement of *mawashi geri* is to lift the knee to the side as the intention is to give it a horizontal or arcing motion for its course. Obviously, the main power of the kick comes from the hip rotation and the reverse rotation of the upper body, which creates a wringing action and then a sharp snap-back of the kick. The hip is totally rotated at the point of impact with the target.

So, we have reviewed the mechanical differences between these two kicks, which will lead you to contemplate why *mikazuki geri* is not used in tournament *kumite*. The answer is very simple, and I am sure the reader can pinpoint the reason.

If you are a tournament competitor, you can easily recognize that this technique is almost impossible to score a point with. It is a *kekomi geri*, so you will be disqualified if you execute a good one to the *jodan*. If you throw it softly, however, you will not get a point. This kick has no snapback; thus, it is very difficult for the judges to determine whether your kick was good or ineffective. Regardless, it is much easier to score a point using *mawashi geri* than *mikazuki geri*, which means the former kick is more effective from a tournament perspective.

Now, here comes a big question: were the Okinawan practitioners unable to do *mawashi geri*, or did they not have such a kick? The ancient Okinawan masters practiced karate for life-or-death combat. Is it, then, difficult to believe that they never practiced *mawashi geri* or that they did not use this kick? I know they knew and practiced it, and I have proof.

I purposely omitted any mention of the *kata* Unsu. This is supposedly the most advanced *kata* of Shotokan. (Some would argue that Hyakuhachiho [百八歩], a forgotten Shotokan *kata* that is also known as *Suparinpei* [スーパーリンペイ] in Shito Ryu and Goju Ryu, is more complex and advanced.) Out of all twenty-six JKA *kata*, Unsu is the only one that has a *mawashi geri* in it.

If you are an advanced practitioner, you know the particular technique I am referring to, which is executed after falling down on the ground. You are lying on your right side, bracing yourself with both forearms on the ground in front of you and kicking to the middle or lower section of the attacker. This is called *deai* (出合い, 'meeting head-on') and is a counter against an attacker who is attacking you with a strong *oi zuki* (追い突き).

I will discuss why *mawashi geri* is used in this context later in this chapter. Let us first examine why the ancient masters did not execute this kick in any other *kata* and kept it as a somewhat hidden technique. Here are a few reasons.

1.   Exposure of the Groin Area

As I have mentioned before, the Okinawan masters did not commonly include

yoko geri in the *kata*. The *yoko geri* you see in Heian Nidan and Heian Yondan were *mae geri* before Funakoshi
changed them. In Shito Ryu, they still use *mae geri* in the
Pin'an *kata*. The reason for avoiding *yoko geri* is the same,
i.e., to avoid exposing the groin area.

2. Visibility

The second-biggest shortcoming of *mawashi geri* is its lack of visibility when
compared to *mae geri* and *mikazuki geri*. To execute a *mawashi geri*, you need to
tuck your knee to the side, which increases visibility significantly. In *budo*, this is
considered to be a bad move.

3. Technical Complexity

The body mechanics of *mawashi geri* are much more complex than those of
mae geri. To explain these mechanics in detail, I would need to use up a great deal
of space, but this chapter is about *mikazuki geri*, not *mawashi geri*, so I will skip
this part of the process here.

4. Secrecy

When investigating Okinawan karate history, we find masters who had the title
Keri no (蹴りの, 'Master of Kicks') attached to their name. A few names of these
keri masters are *Kinjo*, *Kiyatake*, and *Ishimine*. I am sure there were many others,
but, unfortunately, not much written history was left by the ancient Okinawans for
two major reasons, both of which are tied to secrecy.

One reason was the secrecy with regard to the governing Shimazu Clan from
Japan. They had imposed weapons bans upon the native Okinawans, and karate
practice was also prohibited. The other reason was the secrecy with which each

master guarded his techniques from his opponents and from other Okinawa masters.

So, now you see that the Okinawan masters did not want to use *mawashi geri* openly or frequently for the reasons described above. So, let's get back to the earlier question: why is *mawashi geri* used in Unsu, which is supposedly the most advanced *kata* of the JKA?

The key to answering this question is found in the unique execution of the technique. This kick is not executed from a normal stance, such as *zenkutsu dachi*. Rather, you fall to the ground first and then execute this kick from a prone position. So, we must ask a critical question: why would a person fall down like this to execute a kick? Isn't that a crazy move? Give me one convincing reason you need to fall down first before throwing a kick.

You may say, "Hey, it is a surprise technique." But, I must counter by saying, "It is a self-destructive move and not a wise one."

Some readers may say, "From the ground, you can sweep the opponent's leg and take him down. I have seen a demo by Tanaka Sensei where he does that particular technique."

I have seen that demo, too, so your claim is supported, but what I must bring to your attention is how Tanaka Sensei was positioned at the beginning of that demo. He was sitting in *seiza* (正座, 'kneeling position'), not standing. This is a critical point, and it means that he did not need to fall down as he was already down.

He also did the technique differently from the way it is performed in Unsu. Specifically, he was not lying down; he supported his kick by kneeling on his left leg and using his extended left arm to support his leaning upper body while he executed the *mawashi geri*. We must also note that his left forearm was not used to support his upper body as required in this *kata*. These requirements make it very difficult to perform this kick in an effective way.

In Unsu, when you get to the execution of this kick, you realize another very interesting thing. We are told that we are to execute *mawashi geri*, but you will find that it is not a real *mawashi geri* in the strictest sense of the word. It is actually closer to the movement of *mae geri*.

So, what does this mean? This was the typical way in which the ancient masters hid certain techniques in the *kata*. You can practice *bunkai* all you want from the standing position, as it is done in the *kata*, but the real *bunkai* is from the *seiza* position as this is the typical way of sitting in Japan. You will realize that *mae geri* is very hard to execute from *seiza* even though Asai Sensei showed that it can be done. From this position, *mawashi geri* is much easier and much more effective.

Another merit of this execution is how it looks. An outsider would not recognize this kick as a *mawashi geri* just by looking at it as it looks closer to a *mae geri*, so you can hide a *mawashi geri* in this *kata*.

There was no textbook in the nineteenth century to describe each *kata* movement. It was only during the early part of the last century that the late Funakoshi published karate books in which he presented the *kata* with pictures, which resulted in a revolution in karate learning. Up to that point, each move of the *kata*, as well as the *bunkai*, had been taught only through verbal instruction.

Now, let's go back to the very first question: is *mikazuki geri* an extinct kick? By now, you have enough information to know, so I really do not need to answer the question. It is true that in the tournaments I have participated in and observed over many years, I have never seen anyone execute, let alone score a point with, *mikazuki geri* in a *kumite* match. However, what I have witnessed in recent tournaments is a combination of *mae geri* and a smaller version of *mawashi geri*, which is called a *flop kick*.

This flop kick is a little snap kick that is generated by a quick hip vibration and a whipping of the foot, which is very similar to the mechanics used in *mikazuki geri*. Since it is almost impossible to score a point with *mikazuki geri*, tournament fighters have improvised and created a miniature or modified *mawashi geri* that they can score with, especially if they can show a good snapback after the kick.

Even though *mikazuki geri*, in its strictest sense, is not seen or used in *kumite* matches, the mechanics of this kick have been adopted among competitors as I have explained above. Since *mikazuki geri* can be a dangerous kick, it is used only in a defensive movement, such as an arm-slapping block against a *chudan zuki*, if practiced at all.

The real application is not like that at all. It is a stomping kick, typically thrown to *jodan*, which is a knockout kick. The only person who was able to demonstrate this technique well was Asai Sensei. He showed the variety of *furiken* techniques not only with his arms and fists but also with *mikazuki geri* as an attacking technique to *jodan*. *Furiken* is effective and lethal but not commonly practiced in our dojo.

I hope the reader has realized that *mikazuki geri* can be used in a real fighting situation and can have a devastating effect. I also hope the reader will agree that *mikazuki geri* is far from being either an extinct kick or an antique kick that is preserved only in a museum of *kata*. If you have not added *mikazuki geri* to your *kihon* and *kumite*, maybe now you will want to expand your repertoire of kicking techniques.

CHAPTER FIVE
第五章

DISPARITY BETWEEN KATA AND KUMITE
形と組手の関係の謎

Have you ever noticed in our training that there is a big disparity between *kata* and *kumite*? In *kata*, we are taught to always step forward, while we learn to retreat in *kumite* (particularly in *sanbon* and *gohon kumite*). It is true that a few *kata* (of the twenty-six JKA *kata*), such as Jion and Jiin (慈陰), start with a step backward, but it is only one step backward and never three or five.

Of course, one exception is Chinte (珍手). I am aware that the very last three moves of this *kata* are a series of steps, or rather hops, backward. I have written about this *kata* in the past, and I explain in *Shotokan Myths* why we have those mysterious hops in this *kata*. In short, I have concluded from my research that these hops were added in the twentieth century and that the original Chinte, or Chintei, did not have them.

Let's discuss the disparity by explaining *kata*. Heian Shodan is the most basic *kata* (other than Taikyoku), and its moves consist of only forward steps. Even going backward, as with the third step, is done with a 180-degree turn instead of an actual step backward. The most interesting sequence in Heian Shodan is the seventh to ninth steps, where we step forward three times, executing a *jodan age uke* with each step.

Now let's look at *sanbon kumite*. Here we are taught to step backward three times while executing a blocking technique, such as *jodan age uke* or *gedan barai*, with each step. As far as I know, we are not taught to do the reverse. In other words, the attacker delivers a *jodan* or *chudan* punch by stepping back while the defender blocks while stepping forward. If the instructor wants to be creative, I guess it can be done. But, try *sanbon kumite* with a *mae geri* or a *yoko geri* while stepping backward. Does this make any sense? I am sure you will agree that it does not. The idea of an attacker stepping backward in general really does not make sense, and it is not realistic from the perspective of a real fight.

Then, how do we explain this vast difference? *Kata* and *kumite* are said to be the yin and yang of karate. So, one may explain, "We practice stepping forward in *kata*, and we learn to retreat in *kumite*." Others claim *kata* is just a form and is not fit for actual fighting. In fact, some of this latter group have even dropped *kata* from their training menu altogether.

Can these explanations be right? This subject certainly is a mystery, and it must be fully explained. We discuss quite a lot about the history, *bunkai*, and philosophy of *kata* and also about the technical side of *kumite*. But, I have not seen or heard much about the relationship between *kata* and *kumite*.

Have you ever imagined that your *kumite* syllabus could be inappropriate or—God forbid—wrong? Have you ever questioned whether the requirements you have for *kumite* are really valid and useful? In other words, can you comfortably tell me that practicing them will definitely develop your *kumite* skills? Well, we need to do some investigation. I invite you to come along with me as we investigate this mystery together.

Let us look at the official requirements set forth by the Japan Karate Association (JKA). On the following page is a list of the *kumite* requirements taken from the 2009 edition of the JKA's *Karate Techo* (空手手帳).

By the way, this *techo* (手帳, 'notebook') is a very interesting document. It contains not only the exam syllabus but also the names of the high *dan* ranks and country representatives. My copy is in Japanese, but I hear it is also published in English. If you are a JKA member, or if you have a friend in the JKA, I suggest you get hold of a copy. You cannot buy one, so you need someone who is high up in the organization to get you one. Even if it is an old edition, it is worthwhile to review it. I highly recommend it.

OK, here is the JKA *kumite* syllabus in the *Karate Techo*:

- Ninth, eighth, and seventh *kyu*: *gohon kumite* (*jodan* and *chudan*)
- Sixth *kyu*: *ippon kumite* (*jodan* and *chudan*)
- Fifth and fourth *kyu*: *ippon kumite* (*jodan, chudan,* and *mae geri*)
- Third *kyu*: *ippon kumite* (*jodan, chudan, mae geri* and *yoko kekomi*)
- Second *kyu*: *jiyu ippon kumite* (*jodan, chudan, mae geri,* and *yoko kekomi*)
- First *kyu*: *jiyu ippon kumite* (*jodan, chudan, mae geri, yoko kekomi,* and *mawashi geri*)
- *Shodan* and above: *jiyu kumite* (自由組手, 'free sparring')

I am also familiar with the exam syllabi of the JKS and the ISKF. Their syllabi are very similar to that of the JKA (shown above). I can safely say that a similar syllabus is being used by most Shotokan organizations around the world. If the syllabus of your organization happens to be vastly different from this list, then I wish to hear from you. I would like to hear why it is structured differently.

OK, let's get back to our discussion. After reviewing the exam syllabus shown above, do you notice anything strange or wrong with what you see? Here is the big question: do you think this syllabus is wrong? I usually keep the answer to the big question until the end of the chapter, but I am doing something different this time. Hold your breath as I give my answer here.

My years of research into this matter and my fifty years of training have convinced me that the *kumite* syllabus shown above is quite acceptable. In other words, the requirements in the syllabus are the right tools to test *kumite* skills. It is true that you may notice a few strange facts about this syllabus, such as the fact that *mawashi geri* is not required until first *kyu* and a few other odd things, but they are not a big issue. Besides, the syllabus should be used only as a guideline.

The examiner is allowed to make some minor modifications or adjustments as he conducts the examination.

Well, if the exam syllabus is correct, and if we are training under an appropriate program, then does the fault lie with the *kata*? Definitely not! The Okinawan masters would not have valued and practiced the *kata* for hundreds of years if they were meaningless and unusable. It is my hope that what you will find in this chapter will help improve your *kumite* training in a significant way.

Our *kumite* syllabus is correct, but let me ask you another question about our entry-level requirements. Do you practice *sanbon* and *gohon kumite* during your regular training? I am sure your answer is yes, and there's no problem with that if you are an eighth or seventh *kyu*. I say, "Excellent! Keep up the good work."

However, if you are a brown or black belt, then I must tell you that this may be a big problem for your *kumite* training. I can almost hear you say, "What's wrong with my training?" I emphatically state that advanced students must minimize, if not totally avoid, both *sanbon* and *gohon kumite* because this is the major cause of the disparity between *kata* and *kumite*.

Do you believe this? I think I need to further explain so that the reader can judge whether or not my claim makes sense. If you are not satisfied with your *kumite*—and I specifically mean only *jiyu kumite* and *jiyu ippon kumite*—I think it is worth reading the rest of this chapter.

Let us take a close look at the *kihon kumite* training syllabus in our regular training. In *kihon kumite* exercises, we all know that the attacker and the defender face each other at a set distance from which the attacker must take one step forward in order to punch the defender's face or body. We call this *kihon distance*.

There are other *kumite* situations, namely, *keri* (蹴り, 'kicking'), and the point

I am trying to make can be applied to *keri*, but I will use punching in this chapter to explain my point.

The defender starts from a natural stance (*shizentai*). To block the attack, he needs to get into a strong stance, such as a front stance (*zenkutsu dachi*). To get into such a stance, he is taught to step backward. If he instead steps forward into his stance, he will run into the attacker and will not be able to execute the correct block and counterattack. So, the defender is taught to step backward in *gohon kumite* (五本組手, 'five-attack sparring') and *sanbon kumite* (三本組手, 'three-attack sparring') as well as in *ippon kumite* (一本組手, 'single-attack sparring').

We all know this, and, as I said previously, if you are an eighth or seventh *kyu*, there is nothing wrong with this. Beginners have difficulty judging distance and cannot perform the complex movements involved in stepping forward or sideways. You feel comfortable using a motion that has you stepping backward in order to escape an attacker who is stepping toward you. It is a very natural movement, so it makes sense for white belts to do *sanbon kumite* and *gohon kumite* in this manner. Through *kihon kumite*, you can learn the basic *kumite* techniques.

When you become an intermediate student, such as a sixth or fifth *kyu*, your syllabus changes, and you should focus more on *ippon kumite* and less on *sanbon* and *gohon kumite*.

When you reach third *kyu*, brown-belt level, you will finally face *jiyu ippon kumite* (自由一本組手), 'semifree sparring'). There are some challenges to the different *kumite* models you encounter as you move up through the *kihon kumite*. Most students can transition well from *gohon kumite* to *sanbon* and *ippon* until they face *jiyu ippon kumite*.

In *jiyu ippon kumite*, both attacker and defender are free to choose their own distances and move around. This freedom of position and distance is quite different from the other *kihon kumite* models, where the distance is set and rather fixed. Initially, and not surprisingly, brown belts have some difficulty determining proper distance. They now find that the distance of the attacking side can be quite different from that of the defending side.

Also, instead of being limited to one-directional movement, which typically forces the defender to step straight backward to block the technique and then deliver a counterattack, this model allows both opponents to move in any direction. The defender is no longer restricted to backward movement, and the attacker is no longer restricted to forward movement. They can now reverse their movements and even move sideways.

This concept of choosing the right distance and creating a favorite *maai* is totally new and challenging to a freshly promoted third-*kyu* student. Another big difference in *jiyu ippon kumite* is that the defender can move at any time after, during, or even before the attacker moves in with his technique. So, a new element of timing is added to the challenge of selecting the correct distance.

Then, what do new third-*kyu* students do when they are defending? They will, without fail, step backward instead of moving forward or to the side. This is very natural as they have learned to block and counter by stepping backward all throughout the different *kumite* models of *gohon*, *sanbon* and *ippon*. So, the instructor will tell the defenders not to step backward or retreat so much. But, he is asking something very difficult because these students have been brainwashed to step backward as the defender all throughout their former exercises.

Now you may ask, "What is wrong with blocking and countering after you step backward?" Let me answer by asking you this question: did you know that stepping straight backward is the worst option one can choose? If you do not believe this, imagine dodging an oncoming car. What would you do? Would you step backward in line with the car's direction of travel? I am sure you would not. You would want to move out of the way to avoid being run over.

Well, this concept indeed applies to *kumite*, as well, where your opponent is charging at you. Now you can see that it is not such a good idea to step straight backward and receive all the energy and power from the attacker.

We must learn better options, including how to step backward at an angle, how to sidestep, and even how to step forward (although certainly not against a car). The best option is to step forward, but this is technically the most difficult and thus the most advanced option. And, believe it or not, this is what we find in our *kata*, but I will talk about this method later in the chapter.

Now, I see two major problems in our dojo training. One is the sad fact that most instructors do not realize that *kihon kumite*, specifically *sanbon* and *gohon kumite*, must be used only for beginners. I have witnessed in many dojo that these exercises are commonly used with intermediate as well as advanced students. Why does this happen? It is simply because *sanbon* and *gohon kumite* are *kumite* exercises that make it easy for the instructor and students to get a lot of physical exercise. As a result, they get the false notion they had a lot of "good" *kumite* training.

Unfortunately, by repeating this exercise, the notion of stepping backward multiple times gets ingrained into their *kumite* tactics. Consequently, when the students are involved in *jiyu ippon kumite* or even *jiyu kumite*, one side charges in to attack as the other side adopts the tactic of stepping backward to "defend" himself.

The second unfortunate fact that causes this problem is found, believe it or not, in *kihon* practice. If your dojo is of the typical Shotokan style, I imagine your *kihon* practice for advanced students goes something like this. First, you get into a *kamae*, a left *zenkutsu dachi* with a *gedan barai*, and then move to *jiyu na kamae*. The first *kihon* is probably *kizami zuki* (along with a front-foot *yori ashi*), which is followed by *jodan oi zuki*. It is a simple but very popular combination. You step forward and repeat this at least five or six times, depending on how big your dojo is.

Once you run out of floor space, you step backward and execute either *jodan age uke* or another type of *uke* along with a *gyaku zuki*. This type of exercise moves on from *jodan* to *chudan* and then to kicks. But, the general rule is that you execute the attacking techniques as you advance forward and the blocking techniques as you step backward.

Most *kihon* exercises are done in a very linear fashion, moving straight forward and straight backward. This is very similar to the movements found in *kihon kumite*. So, the idea of stepping backward when you block is repeatedly reinforced. If your instructor gives you a lot of zigzagging, sidestepping, and *tenshin* exercises in *kihon*, then you are lucky. Unfortunately, I have rarely seen this type of *kihon* training in most of the dojo and seminars I have visited.

OK, let's tackle the best option in *kumite*, namely, stepping forward to defend, which is what we find in all the *kata* we know. Why do you think the Okinawan masters formulated the *kata* this way? It is simply because they believed that moving forward was the best option; therefore, they never included multiple steps backward in any of the *kata*. Stepping straight backward is an option, so we see a backward step in Jion and Jutte, but it is only one step.

Look at Heian Shodan's sixth movement, the left *gedan barai*, followed by the three consecutive *jodan age uke*. Let me explain the *bunkai* for these techniques.

1. Left *gedan barai* (from a left *zenkutsu dachi*): This technique is in response to a right *chudan oi zuki* or right *mae geri* attack.

2. Left *jodan shuto age uke* (remaining in position): This technique is in response to the attacker's right *jodan zuki* or left *jodan gyaku zuki*.

3. Right *age uke* (stepping forward): Even though this technique is called an *uke*, the application is that of an attack. First, your left *shuto* grabs the opponent's wrist and pulls him toward you, which throws off his balance. Then, you use your right *kentsui* (拳槌, 'hammer fist') to strike the opponent's neck or the area under his

chin. This technique can also be a right *mawashi uchi* (回し打ち, 'round-house punch') to the opponent's head (aimed at the temple).

You do this same technique (*jodan age uke*) three times to practice three different counterattacks, and they are not blocking techniques. In *kata*, the defender is taught to always step forward. We know why, and the answer is critically important. You get the most power when you leverage your forward-moving acceleration to aid your attacking techniques.

It is like sticking your fist out of a car. You drive a car at, say, 30 mph (roughly 48 km/h). If your punching speed is, say, rather slow at 5 mph (roughly 8 km/h), then your punch when thrown from a car would be around 35 mph (roughly 56 km/h), an incredible seven times faster than the speed of your punch by itself.

If you step backward, then you must stop before launching a counterattack, so you cannot leverage your forward movement to aid your punch. Thus, your punching speed would be only 5 mph (roughly 8 km/h).

Besides speed, there is also the power of momentum that goes along with forward movement. You get none of this when moving backward. If you deliver a counterattack while stepping backward, your punching or kicking speed is negated by the speed of the backward movement. In addition, you tend to lean back, and this requires you to coil forward again before you can block or counterattack. This action requires more time and slows you down. As far as I know, all other styles, such as Goju Ryu, Shito Ryu, Uechi Ryu (上地流), Ryuei Ryu (劉衛流), etc., share this same concept in their *kata*.

左端の方は船越義珍師範

Now we must look at the history of modern-day karate to understand what has happened to karate as we know it. By studying the history, we will find out how and why the original Okinawan karate has changed and why we have this huge disparity between *kata* and *kumite/kihon.*

No Shotokan karate practitioner will disagree that we have three main elements in our training, and they are *kihon, kumite,* and *kata.* Of course, some people may include other exercises, such as stretches or the muscle exercises known as *hojo keiko* (補助稽古, 'supplementary training'), but the core of the training consists of the three elements I have mentioned above.

Was karate training carried out this way a hundred years ago on Okinawa? Many readers may already know that it was not. Funakoshi, the founder of Shotokan, did not learn karate in this manner when he studied under Azato and Itosu in the late nineteenth century. Azato and Itosu taught Funakoshi only *kata.* The *kihon* and *kumite* exercises, as we know them today, were nonexistent. The teachers, of course, taught Funakoshi *bunkai* applications but no *kihon kumite,* such as *gohon kumite* or even *jiyu kumite,* none whatsoever. *Kihon* and *kumite* were invented and introduced by Funakoshi after he immigrated to Tokyo, Japan, in the early twentieth century. I am sure you are curious as to how and why this change, or new addition, occurred.

Many people know that Funakoshi started teaching at the universities in Tokyo. He could not afford to establish an independent dojo for many years for both financial and political reasons (relating mainly to Kodokan Judo). So, he started with the college karate club idea and taught at many universities as the young men there were very curious about this foreign martial art from Okinawa. Okinawa had just become a new prefecture of Japan, but it was still considered foreign by most mainland Japanese people.

For the first several years, he taught only *kata,* just the way he had been taught on Okinawa. Naturally, those hotheaded university boys were not satisfied with just *kata* training. They wanted to use karate techniques in real fights, and they wanted to do *jiyu kumite.* Funakoshi prohibited all sparring and certainly street fighting. But, the students were not convinced, and they began to

doubt the effectiveness techniques that were only drilled through *kata*. Some of the students challenged Funakoshi and asked if *kumite* was taught on Okinawa, maybe secretly or only to very advanced students. Funakoshi emphatically told them no. He said that only *kata* was taught and that the meaning of the movements was explained by *bunkai*.

They eventually started practicing free sparring, but very secretly. However, one day Funakoshi caught some students free sparring. In fact, he got so upset that he resigned from his teaching position at this university dojo.

At another university, some students took a long trip from Tokyo to Okinawa—this would have taken many days at that time—to double-check how karate was being taught on the island. They found that it was true that Okinawan practitioners did not have *kumite* or *kihon* in their training menu. As a result, some of the more creative students took some training ideas from kendo and judo. From kendo, they introduced free sparring with full protective gear. This developed into a new style known as *Nippon Kempo* (日本拳法), founded in 1932 by Muneomi Sawayama (澤山宗海, 1906–1977). Note that this differs from the style known as *Nihon Kenpo Karatedo* (日本拳法空手道), which was founded in 1959 by Tatsuo Yamada (山田辰雄, 1905–1967).

It is also true that Funakoshi had a close relationship with the founder of Muso Shinden Ryu Iaido (夢想神伝流居合道), Hakudo Nakayama (中山博道, 1872–1958), who was no relation to Masatoshi Nakayama of the JKA. He was very well known among the martial artists of Japan as he was the only person to have received both *judan* (十段, 'tenth degree') and *hanshi* (範士, 'master instructor') ranks in kendo, iaido, and jodo (杖道) from the All Japan Kendo Federation. Hakudo saw Funakoshi's demonstration in Tokyo and was so impressed that he let him use his dojo to teach karate. So, it is very natural to imagine that Funakoshi had a lot of exposure to kendo and its training methods.

As everyone knows, Funakoshi had to depend on the support of Kano, the founder of Kodokan Judo. Kano was probably the most influential figure not only in the martial arts world but also in all athletic events and sports as he was the first

Asian member of the International Olympic Committee (IOC), serving from 1909 to 1938. In fact, he died at sea while returning to Japan from Egypt after attending an IOC conference in Cairo.

Kano was someone who could not be ignored if one wished to start any kind of martial arts or sports activities, let alone a dojo. Kano was so interested in karate after seeing Funakoshi's demonstration that he visited Okinawa himself and spent two full days with Kenwa Mabuni, the founder of Shito Ryu, and Chojun Miyagi (宮城長順, 1888–1953), the founder of Goju Ryu (剛柔流), learning techniques and exchanging martial arts ideas.

Ryuso Kenwa Mabuni

Kenwa Mabuni   Chojun Miyagi

Some of Funakoshi's students came from judo, and it is natural to suspect that they tried to introduce an idea from judo called *randori* (乱取り), a type of freestyle training exercise for throws in which two practitioners work as a pair. Funakoshi accepted many ideas from judo, such as the *karategi* and *obi*—the Okinawans practiced in their street clothes or just in pants—however, he refused to adopt the idea of *randori*.

He instead adopted a training method from kendo called *uchikomi* (打ち込み), a basic striking practice. In this exercise, one practitioner steps forward and throws a series of strikes at the opponent as you would do in *gohon kumite*. But, the big difference is that the kendo opponent does not block or counter. The opponent simply steps back as the attacker advances, so he just presents himself as a target.

Our *kihon kumite* was developed in such a way that a certain technique is called out, and the attacker steps forward with one, three, or five steps as he delivers this attacking technique. The defender, on the other hand, steps backward as he delivers his blocking technique and, on the last step (i.e., the third step in *sanbon kumite* and the fifth step in *gohon kumite*), executes a counterattack after the final block. This is exactly how our *kihon kumite* came about.

If the ancient masters believed that the best moves for attack and defense were those that moved forward, why do we have this problem now? It certainly was not Funakoshi Sensei's or Nakayama Sensei's fault. They developed a curriculum that was appropriate for students of different levels. I believe Funakoshi Sensei taught Nakayama Sensei this concept correctly.

Look, the early JKA successfully produced many *kumite* greats who were exceptionally skillful, such as Oishi, Asai, Kanazawa, Enoeda, Tanaka, and Yahara, to name a few. In addition, by looking at the JKA's *kumite* syllabus, I can say that Nakayama knew how *kumite* was to be developed among his students.

Then, why are we not following this syllabus in our training? We are aware that some of the true *bunkai* for many *kata* have been forgotten. This disparity between *kata* and *kumite* is another mystery. I can only say that the teaching of forward movement has not been emphasized enough in the training of instructors. As a result, the current instructors are teaching classes incorrectly without knowing what they are doing.

You may be wondering, then, whether or not this is a serious error. Well, it depends. This error will not harm anyone physically. It is not like an incorrect kick, which could hurt one's knee or back. This error is hard to get rid of because no one complains. However, many advanced students face difficulties in doing *bunkai* correctly as most of them require a forward-stepping motion. They also find themselves having difficulty when they transition to *jiyu ippon kumite* and *jiyu kumite*.

So, what must we do, then? If you are an instructor, you must stop using *sanbon* and *gohon kumite* with your advanced students. Instead, have them do more *ippon kumite* and *jiyu ippon kumite* to prepare for *jiyu kumite*. Additionally, teach students the sidestepping and forward-stepping techniques. Require them to do these techniques and discourage movements that go straight backward. On the other hand, if you are an advanced student (a brown belt or, particularly, a *shodan* or *nidan*), practice more *jiyu ippon kumite* and use those techniques to step forward rather than backward when you are on the defending side. So, the key words are *step forward*.

I hope my advice will help you in your *kumite* training. You will not know until you try. If you are not satisfied with what you are doing in *kumite* right now, you have nothing to lose by trying this out. You may find that your poor performance is not because of a lack of ability; it may, in fact, be due to incorrect *kumite* practice routines.

OK, I may have been a little too optimistic with my statement that "you have nothing to lose." You may get your nose punched in or take a kick to your midsection as you try to step in. So, there is that risk in this approach, but I strongly recommend that you try it as it is worth the risk. I hope you agree as it could mean a significant improvement in your *kumite* skills. Believe me, your counterattacks will be far more powerful, and your opponents will find that your techniques are significantly harder to dodge or block. In addition, you will be able to understand the *bunkai* better and more easily. As you become more familiar with these movements, it will be easier for you to execute the *bunkai* techniques. I believe it is about time we give credit to our *kata*, which has made karate a unique *bujutsu* (武術, 'martial art').

So, we have learned why we have this big disparity between *kata* and *kumite*. If you are an advanced student and wish to develop your *kumite* as a potent martial arts skill, I urge you to minimize your practice of *sanbon* and *gohon kumite* and

to increase your practice of forward-moving techniques in *ippon kumite* and *jiyu ippon kumite*.

I would be happy to hear that this chapter has helped the individual practitioner, but I wrote it mainly for instructors. If we are going to reduce the disparity that clearly exists in our current training, shouldn't the correction be initiated and implemented by the instructors? I urge instructors to examine their teaching syllabus not only in the *kumite* portion but also in the areas of *kihon* and *kata* so that there will be consistency within the entire training program.

The main message I wish to leave with the reader is that retreating or stepping backward is an option, but it is the worst option, so do not retreat in *kumite*. You must always think of advancing forward, as you do in *kata*.

押忍

CHAPTER SIX
第六章

WHY UCHI UKE?
内受けの謎

Have you ever noticed that there are only two outside blocks in all of the five Heian *kata* combined? One is found in Heian Sandan, and the other in Heian Godan.
All the other blocks in the Heian *kata* are inside blocks, such as *gedan barai, uchi
ude uke, age uke,* and *shuto uke.* Does it matter, or should we even care about this?
I think we should.

When I noticed this, I found it very puzzling because I know that outside
blocks, in general, are much easier to execute than inside blocks. For instance,
chudan soto uke (中段外受け) is very popular in *kihon* practice as well as in *kihon
kumite* (e.g., *ippon kumite, sanbon kumite,* etc.), but, strangely, it is not found in
our basic Heian *kata.* So, I wondered about this for a long time but could not ask
my sensei or *senpai* as this subject seemed to be too trivial. I finally found the
answer on my own when I became a more senior practitioner and began to understand *budo* karate. Let us look into this, and I will share what I have discovered.

Uchi Uke (内受け, 'Inside Blocks')

First, let's look at the definition of an inside
block. This is a blocking method in which the
blocking arm is pulled in toward the inside of the
body before it travels toward the outside. On the
other hand, an outside block is where the blocking
arm is initially brought toward the outside of the
body before it travels inward. We will discuss inside blocks first and then cover outside blocks later.

Let's review all the *uke waza* in the Heian *kata.* In Heian Shodan, we see *gedan barai, jodan age uke,* and *shuto uke,* which are all *uchi uke.*

In Heian Nidan, we have *age uke* or *jodan ude uke, shuto uke, chudan osae
uke, chudan uchi ude uke, gedan barai,* and the last move, which is *jodan age uke.*
These blocks are also all *uchi uke.*

Some interpret the second move in Heian Nidan as a *hasami uke* (鋏受け)

using both arms. Any technique that works is acceptable for *bunkai*, but Heian Nidan was Pin'an Shodan, and I doubt very much that Itosu would introduce such a unique technique into the first *kata*. I have seen such an application in a Hong Kong kung fu movie, but it definitely looked artificial rather than practical.

In Heian Sandan, the *uke waza* are *chudan uchi ude uke, morote kosa uke, chudan ude uke, chudan osae uke, soto enpi uke*, and *chudan tsukami uke*. As I mentioned earlier, Heian Sandan has one outside block, *soto enpi uke*, but all the other blocks are inside blocks.

How about Heian Yondan, which is a more complex *kata*? The blocks are *jodan shuto uke, gedan kosa uke, chudan uchi ude uke, shuto gedan barai, jodan shuto age uke, morote uchi kakiwake* (諸手内掻き分け), and *chudan shuto uke*. Again, these are all inside blocks, and no outside blocks are used.

Is it the same with Heian Godan? Let's check. The blocks in this *kata* are *chudan uchi ude uke, gedan kosa uke, jodan shuto kosa uke, gedan barai, chudan haishu uke* (中段背手受け), *jodan kaishu nagashi uke* (上段開手流し受け), and *manji uke*. *Jodan kaishu nagashi uke*, which is found twice in this *kata*, is an outside block, but this is the only exception. All the other blocks are inside blocks.

We have confirmed that only two blocks out of those found in all the Heian *kata* are outside blocks. Now let's look at our *kihon kumite* and see what kind of blocks we use. In our *ippon* and *sanbon kumite*, we frequently see *soto ude uke* at both *jodan* and *chudan* levels. You are not only allowed but often instructed to use these blocks despite the fact that we do not see them in the Heian *kata*. This is what is mysterious and puzzling, at least to me.

Let's look back to the time when Itosu created Heian *kata* in the late nineteenth century. Did you know that the training syllabus then was strictly *kata* only? The instructors might have shown the *bunkai* to the most senior students, but there was no *kihon kumite* training in Okinawan karate at that time. For that matter, there wasn't even any *kihon* training that consisted of doing one technique repeatedly up and down the dojo. In fact, both *kihon* training and *kihon kumite* training were added after Funakoshi came to Japan.

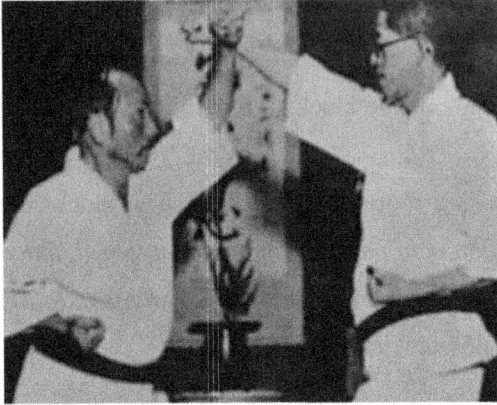

How and when exactly they were introduced is not known or documented, but it is a documented fact that many of the university students showed great dissatisfaction with the *kata*-only training of Funakoshi in the 1920s. Some of them visited Okinawa to examine how karate was taught where it had come from. In order to learn more about the training syllabus, some, including Otsuka (a student of Funakoshi and the subsequent founder of Wado Ryu), visited other karate instructors who had moved to Japan from Okinawa, such as Motobu and Mabuni, who had both moved to Osaka in 1921 and 1929, respectively.

As I mentioned in Chapter 1, Otsuka departed from Funakoshi somewhere between 1929 and 1930, after having trained under him for only a few years. My understanding is that Otsuka and the university students requested a *kumite* training syllabus, which forced Funakoshi to add regimented training methods for *kihon kumite*, such as *sanbon kumite*, *gohon kumite*, etc.

It is known that a strong influence came from kendo training. The Okinawan masters never believed in the retreating movements that are found in *kihon kumite*, particularly those of *sanbon* and *gohon kumite*. This is why you never see any multiple steps backward in our *kata*. The moves are, in general, either straight forward or to the sides.

If this is the case in our *kata*, we must ask ourselves why our *kihon kumite* always has the defender stepping backward. Just watch the *kihon* training of kendo, and you will see that its practitioners move straight forward and backward in a very linear fashion. The adoption of this training is what caused the great disparity between *kata* and *kihon kumite*. I discussed this subject in the previous chapter, so I will not repeat it here.

After practicing *kihon kumite* so much, becoming comfortable with stepping backward, and using mainly *soto uke*, many students began to believe that *kata* techniques, and *kata* as a whole, did not work. Some of them dropped the *kata* from their training syllabus entirely. The *kata* were created by the masters of the past, who developed them from actual fighting experiences, or so we've been told. So, we must ask, "Does *kata* work in a real fighting situation?" My short answer is "Yes." My longer answer is "Yes, but you need to know the *bunkai*."

Most of the *bunkai* techniques cannot be practiced in the three- or five-step linear movements that we do in *kihon kumite*. The *bunkai* are much more complex in their footwork, *taisabaki*, etc. If this is the case, then do we need *kihon kumite*? Yes, I believe we do. I wrote about this particular subject in the previous chapter, so I will not cover it in depth here, but the two major benefits that I can see in *kihon kumite* are the chance to practice *maai* (間合い, 'distance') and the simple act of facing an opponent. These two things are very hard to learn from practicing only *kata*.

Let us get back to what we were discussing: the *uke waza* in the Heian *kata*. Itosu, the creator of Heian, obviously believed that the *uchi uke* were more important and necessary than the *soto uke*. *Chudan uchi ude uke* and *chudan shuto uke* are difficult to use, especially when you retreat straight backward. All you have to do is to try these techniques in *sanbon kumite*, and you will see. These difficult blocks, *shuto uke* and *uchi ude uke*, finally start to work well once you begin shifting your body on the angles in your *kumite*.

So, we now realize that some of the *uchi uke* work better when we move on the angles. But, you may ask why the outside blocks are ignored or unused in *kata*. As I studied further into *bunkai*, I came up with two good reasons. A hint is that the Okinawan masters were hard-core martial artists.

The first reason is that they despised techniques that would expose the vital points of the body. This was the very reason they did not include *mawashi geri* and *yoko geri keage* when they created the *kata*. These kicks would obviously expose the groin area, which was something to be avoided completely. The other vital areas are the solar plexus (*chudan* level) and the eyes, temples, throat, etc. (*jodan* level).

If you understand this concept, then it is easy to see that the masters believed it was almost suicidal to swing an arm way outside of the body's center line to prepare for a block. We were taught in our training some fifty years ago to always "hide" the vital points, which run mostly along the *chushinsen* (中心線), or *seichu-sen* (正中線), an imaginary line that runs from the top of the head to the tailbone. If you examine the only two outside blocks found in the Heian *kata*, *soto enpi uke* and *jodan teisho nagashi uke*, more closely, you will realize that neither block requires an arm to be swung outwardly.

By the way, the *soto enpi uke* seen in Heian Sandan is interesting, to say the least. You might be wondering why, if the masters so disliked exposing the *chushinsen* to their opponents, they would use a stance that places their fists on their hips like Superman, which exposes so much of their front. There is an Okinawan custom behind this technique that is not well known. The clothes of the Okinawan *bushi* (武士, 'warrior' or 'samurai') had openings near the hips (almost like pockets), and they customarily kept their hands inside these openings even when they walked, just as you might walk with your hands in your pockets. Therefore, standing in this position was very normal to the Okinawan masters.

The second reason the ancient masters did not focus on *soto uke* (blocking techniques in which the blocking arm travels from the outside to the inside of the body's center line, the mechanism of which is described in detail below) may be the following.

Including the unique *soto enpi uke* (shown below), all *soto uke* utilize the mechanism of muscle contraction. This contraction is mainly used to pull something or someone toward oneself. This type of mechanism is important in sports such as judo and wrestling. In karate, on the other hand, we punch and kick, which requires the expansion of the body.

Of course, when we expand our arm or leg, there is naturally some contraction of the muscles. However, we all know that relaxation is an important part of being able to strike or kick quickly. If the muscles are unnecessarily contracted during a punch or kick, the technique will be slow and jerky.

This may be the second reason the ancient masters minimized the use of blocking techniques that require contraction of the muscles. The use of *uchi uke*, on the other hand, was maximized as these are blocking techniques that utilize the expansion of our limbs.

Soto Uke (外受け, 'Outside Blocks')

In the Heian *kata*, there are only two outside blocks, which I have mentioned previously.

Soto Enpi Uke (外猿臂受け) in Heian Sandan

This block is used not only in Heian Sandan but also in Gankaku. From a mechanical perspective, it is an outside block, but the blocking arm is not pulled out. In fact, the arm is stable as the fists are attached to the hips.

In Heian Sandan, naturally, *kiba dachi* is used, and this is a very reasonable tactic as you need to minimize the exposure of the front of your body. We also see this block in Gankaku, and the difference there is that it is done from *shizentai* with quick hip rotations. But, the ba-

sic idea is the same as in Heian Sandan.

Jodan Teisho Nagashi Uke (上段底掌流し受け) in Heian Godan

This is a very popular technique that is found not
only in Heian Godan but also in Bassai and Kanku. The
upper arm is a *jodan nagashi uke*, and the lower arm is
a *gedan* attack with a *shuto*. As you practice these *kata*,
you will notice that the move just before the *jodan nagashi uke* is typically a *gedan barai*. In other words, that
arm is kept low and not moved outward, which would
expose the front of the body. Though the arm does travel
from the outside to the inside, the technique essentially moves from the front of the
body toward the back, passing the head.

This move is definitely quite different from a typical *chudan soto ude uke*. The
outside-to-inside movement is very subtle, and the exposure of the body is minimal. I am sure you can understand why the *kata* creators included this technique.
Now let us look at the other outside blocks we learn in *kihon* and *kumite*.

Chudan Soto Ude Uke (中段外腕受け)

Probably the most popular blocking technique against a *chudan oi zuki* in *sanbon* or *gohon kumite* is the *chudan soto ude uke*. As the attacker steps in with a
chudan oi zuki, the defender brings his blocking arm wide and high over his shoulder just as a bird would spread its wing. Then, he brings that arm around almost
horizontally in a semicircular motion and blocks the punch with his forearm.

Though this is the most popular block, we do not find it in the Heian *kata*. We
see it for the first time in Bassai Dai. Why is this? There must be a reason. What
is wrong with this block? Well, nothing is "wrong" with it, but there are two facts
about it that the Okinawan masters did not like.

One is the fact that this block takes more time to throw than an *uchi uke* because of the longer path the blocking arm must travel to execute it. This is because it must be pulled back before it goes forward to block. Secondly, and more importantly, by bringing the blocking arm outward, you expose your midsection even if you try to cover it with the other arm. From a martial artist's perspective, this is something you want to avoid.

In the *kata*, these moves are called *soto ude uke*, and they are performed as if they were blocks. However, the *soto ude uke* in Bassai Dai are not really blocks. If you study the *bunkai* for these moves, you will realize that they are actually throws.

What makes me laugh is that some people really believe one popular interpretation of these combinations. In this interpretation, it is explained that the two *soto ude uke* thrown in succession are used to switch the blocking hand in order to gain a favorable position. It does not take an intelligent or high-ranking individual to realize that this is an unrealistic, and frankly ridiculous, move. Just think. If you are the attacker, and you have just thrown an *oi zuki*, would you be standing still with your arm extended after your attack is blocked long enough for your opponent to switch arms? If you are that slow, maybe you should give up practicing karate.

It really makes sense, though, if you introduce the concept of throwing for those moves. Try this *bunkai* idea, and see if it makes sense.

Jodan Soto Ude Uke (上段外腕受け)

We find this block only in Unsu and Jutte (Jitte). In Unsu, it is thrown very quickly from a one-legged stance after a *mae geri* and a fast body rotation. It is then followed by a *chudan gyaku zuki*. This *kata* is considered to be among those of the highest skill level in Shotokan.

It is interesting that we find *jodan soto ude uke* in Unsu, but it is even more interesting that we also find it in Jutte. In the latter, you raise both arms up over your shoulders in a U shape above your head. You keep this shape as you execute the outside forearm block. As you move from one *kiba dachi* to another, you rotate both arms around.

We find this to be a strange move until we learn that this *kata* was based on fighting with or against a *bo* (棒, 'staff'). This swinging movement in which both hands are held above the head is no longer unnatural or strange once you imagine that you are holding a staff above your head. Therefore, we must say that what we see in Jutte is actually not a *jodan soto ude uke*. We must conclude that this block is found only in Unsu.

Let's look at the other JKA *kata* and see what other outside blocks we can find.

Jodan Teisho Uke (上段底掌受け) in Gankaku

This technique has caused much debate when it comes to *bunkai*. The combination is performed as a double-handed block: a *haishu uke* with the left hand and a *teisho uke* with the right hand. So, it can be considered a combination of an *uchi uke* and a *soto uke*.

However, I believe this technique used to be a *kosa uke* just like the one found in Heian Godan. It is followed by a *tsukami uke* with a rotation of the wrists and then a *nihon zuki*, exactly the way it is done in Heian Godan. I suspect Itosu took these moves from Gankaku when he created Heian Godan.

Nevertheless, this is not pertinent to the discussion we are having here. It is OK even if the right hand is a *soto teisho uke* as this pressing block is done quickly, and the right arm is not brought way outside of the body's center line, as we see in *soto ude uke*.

Gedan Soto Ude Uke (下段外腕受け) in Tekki Nidan

This technique is found in the fourth and eighth moves of Tekki Nidan, and these are the only two places we find this outside block in the entire *kata* syllabus. This move could be a *soto ude uke* against a *mae geri* or a *chudan zuki*, but, at the same time, it could also be interpreted as a breakaway technique from a wrist grab.

Another interesting interpretation has the open hand supporting the elbow of the *soto uke* arm, but we will not go into this here. I plan to write a chapter on Tekki Nidan and Tekki Sandan in the future.

Chudan Teisho Uke (中段底掌受け) in Jion, Jutte, and Chinte

This technique is thrown from *kiba dachi* in Jion and Jutte. So, it is very natural and makes sense as this allows you to keep the narrowest profile possible when facing the opponent in this stance. Your blocking hand is held at the hip until the last moment and is delivered very quickly without bringing the forearm very far outside of the body's center line.

In Chinte, it is thrown from *sochin dachi*, and the technique is executed with the right and left hands operating in succession, which means that the first one is used to block a *chudan zuki*, and the second one follows up with a strike to the elbow.

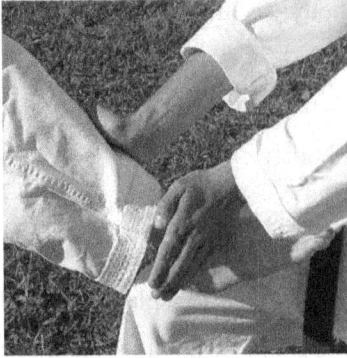

Morote teisho uke is used at the very end of Hangetsu. Yes, it is possible to use this technique against *mae geri*, as shown in the photo to the left, but this is not a realistic application as you are totally exposing your face to the kicker, who will punch to *jodan* as soon as his kick is blocked like this.

I believe I mentioned this in my previous book, *Shotokan Myths*, under Chapter 11: "Hangetsu," but Funakoshi changed this from the original technique, which was *morote mawashi uke*, to the current technique. My research has not yet discovered for what reason or benefit he made this change. All I can say is that this is a strange technique to end a *kata* with because, contrary to popular belief, *kata* do not end with blocks.

Note that there are many other kinds of *uke* other than *soto uke* and *uchi uke*. Some move upward (*keito uke* [鶏頭受け]), downward (*osae uke* [押さえ受け] or *otoshi uke* [落し受け]), or in a circle (*kaiten uke* [回転受け]). Some rotate (*mawashi uke* [回し受け]), and some even move forward (*tome waza* [止め技]) or back toward oneself (*nagashi uke* [流し受け]).

Conclusion

As we have reviewed both *uchi uke* and *soto uke*, we have realized that the *kata* creators obviously wanted to keep the arms inside and did not include any blocks that would bring the arms way outside of the body's center line. From a martial arts perspective, this is only natural, and there is nothing to debate.

As I close this chapter, I want to reiterate an important fact about karate tech-

niques that may not be very obvious. As previously discussed, most karate techniques are all about the expansion of the muscles. This is a big contrast to the
techniques of judo, which mainly consist of contraction, or pulling inward. On the
other hand, you can easily see that karate strikes and kicks mainly consist of expansion, or stretching your muscles outward. Of course, there are some contraction
techniques, such as *ushiro enpi uchi* (後ろ猿臂打ち), *kagi zuki*, and *ura mawashi
geri* (裏回し蹴り), but these techniques are in the minority.

We tend to forget this as we introduce the concept of *kime* (極め), particularly
in our punching techniques. I have already written on the harmful side of *kime* in
Chapter 1: "Kime" of my previous book, *Shotokan Myths*, so I will not repeat it
here. However, I must end this chapter with a remark that modern Shotokan has
forgotten the concept of ki flow as it relates to the delivery of a technique. Too
much *kime* stops or prevents ki flow or energy flow, thus making the technique
ineffective and the performer stiff and rigid.

押忍

CHAPTER SEVEN
第七章

DOES SHOTOKAN LACK CIRCULAR TECHNIQUES?
松濤館と直線技の謎

I often hear the comment that Shotokan karate lacks circular movements and techniques. Some claim that other styles, such as Goju Ryu and Uechi Ryu, have more circular techniques. I hear this not only from practitioners of styles other than Shotokan but also from the instructors of Shotokan itself. If the instructors feel this way, then it must be true. Or is it? Before believing this theory, we must do some investigation.

The most popular attacking technique in Shotokan is *choku zuki* (直突き, 'straight punch'). It is very true that a *choku zuki* travels a very straight path (as shown in the photo to the left). Your teacher tells you to keep the elbow in and down so that your punch will not make an arc.

So, you might say, "*Oi zuki* and *gyaku zuki* are very popular in Shotokan, so our attacking techniques look straight." You are absolutely correct about one thing, and that is the word *look*. The fist's line of travel is indeed straight. We will discuss this point further later on.

The abovementioned mechanism also applies to *yoko geri kekomi*. In this kick, the kicking foot, after being tucked up near the opposite knee, will indeed travel straight to the target (or at least it's supposed to).

Besides these "straight" techniques, our *kata*'s *enbusen* (演武線) are very linear, a combination of straight lines crossed by either forty-five- or ninety-degree angles. In addition to *kata*, our *kumite* syllabus, such as *sanbon kumite* and *gohon kumite*, ingrains into our brain the idea that our moves must be very straight and linear. Considering these points, it's no wonder our karate looks linear. We will discuss these two points, *kata* and *kumite*, more in depth later in this chapter.

Let us get back to the discussion of karate techniques. Here, we must look more deeply into the physical mechanics of our body. What goes on behind the scenes is a combination of the turning of the shoulder socket and the circular movement of the upper arm as the punch is delivered. So, the elbow swings like a pendulum as you extend your punching arm, and that is a circular movement.

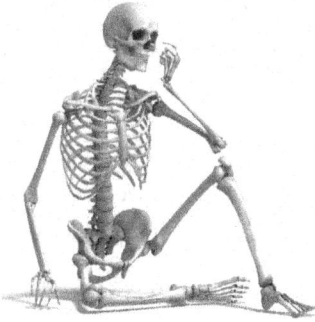

This is the basic concept of the physiological mechanics of our body. We are all aware that our body is constructed of many sticks (bones) and the joints (knees, elbows, etc.) that connect them. This means that all the complex body movements we make in our daily lives, such as walking, shaking hands, and eating, are made up of the straight and circular movements of these sticks. Of course, some of these movements are more complex and sophisticated, but, in general, these two motions are the basis of all our body movements. If this is the case with our normal daily activities, then it is easily guessed that all karate techniques require some kind of circular movement.

You can review all the "straight" techniques in every punch, kick, and block, and you will see that these techniques require some combination of straight and circular movements. In other words, these techniques use the circular movements of the arms (including the shoulders) and the legs (including the hips), and there are even some circular movements that use hip rotation (as in *gyaku zuki*). This covers not only Shotokan karate but also a much broader spectrum, which includes all karate styles, all martial arts, and all athletic and physical activities.

Believe it or not, we already have many techniques in Shotokan that are very circular. An excellent example that we all know is *shuto uchi* (手刀打ち, 'knife-hand strike'). Let's take a closer look. The illustration shown to the right

definitely shows the circular movement of this technique. We find this technique once in Heian Yondan and many times in Kanku Dai, so it is a very familiar technique to us. The illustration of *shuto uchi* shows an inward swing, but this technique can also be applied with an outward swing. In fact, we practice a technique called *shuto uke* (手刀受け, 'knife-hand block') very frequently. Even though the outward movement does not travel a large circular path, it is still a circular technique, and we start practicing this technique as early as when we begin our first *kata*, Heian Shodan.

Let's look at the kicking techniques next. The most popular kick in Shotokan is *mae geri*. Many people believe it is a straight kick because in *mae geri kekomi* (前蹴り蹴込み, 'front thrust kick'), the foot does move straight forward (Picture 1). But if you look at the mechanics of this kick more closely, you will notice that it is definitely a circular kick and not a linear technique (Picture 2).

1   2

When you think of a circular kick, *mawashi geri* will most likely come to mind. We all agree that the movement of this kick is very circular. I am sure you were taught to bring the kicking knee up to hip height and then deliver the kick horizontally in a very circular way. You were also told to rotate not only the kicking leg but the entire hip area along with it. We can also say that other kicks, such as *yoko geri keage* and *mikazuki geri*, must be considered circular techniques, as well.

Earlier we discussed that *shuto uke* is a circular move. How about other blocks? Let's look at two very popular blocks, *chudan soto ude uke* (Picture 3) and *age uke* (Picture 4), which are shown in the illustrations below. These two blocks are definitely circular in their movements. As a matter of fact, if you examine the motions of other blocks, such as *chudan uchi uke* and *gedan barai*, you will find that they also move in a circular way, though this may not be as obvious as in *soto uke*.

3   4

We have looked at quite a few popular techniques, and you must admit that all our techniques employ circular movements. Well, you might say, "OK, I agree that these techniques are supposed to be circular, but our moves do not look circular." Well, I think you hit the bull's eye. This impression may well be the exact reason many readers feel that Shotokan karate lacks circular movements.

Now it looks as though we are back to square one, and here I challenge you by asking this key question: why must our techniques look circular? You must believe a circular movement is better than a straight one as you ascribe much value to circular techniques, so we must know why. Let us examine circular techniques and see if there are any significant merits to support your beliefs. Below are three popular advantages of circular movements.

1. Circular movements allow for an easier transition from one technique to another as the completion of one technique blends into the initiation of

the one that follows. In other words, a series of movements can be made without stopping between each one.

2. Circular movements use a whiplike motion (as in *uraken uchi*, *shuto uchi*, *mawashi geri*, etc.), which allows them to generate a lot of speed and power as they hit the target.

3. Circular movements look smoother than straight ones, whereas our techniques give the impression of rigid or jerky motions.

Next let's review each of these advantages more in depth.

1. Easier Transitions

This is probably the biggest reason we believe a circular motion is better than a linear one. In a circular motion, one technique can lead into another without stopping or slowing down. A good example may be a combination of a *jodan shuto age uke* and a *jodan shuto soto mawashi uchi* using the same arm. This shows that one movement or an action could contain two, three, or even more techniques.

This is extremely difficult to get from a linear technique. It can be done with two techniques packed into one motion—a *yama zuki*, for instance, may be considered a simultaneous *jodan uke* and *jodan zuki*—but having three or four is almost impossible.

2. More Speed and Power

It is true that a whiplike motion can create tremendous speed at the end of its travel, a point that can be proven by a real whip. However, from a scientific point of view, a circular motion takes more time to arrive at its target than a straight one does (provided these actions move at the same speed).

No one would dispute the fact that the distance of a circular movement is greater than that of a straight line. A straight punch will reach the target sooner than the long swing of a *shuto* or backfist (again, assuming that the speed of the techniques is the same). So, a circular movement is not necessarily a better solution when you are talking about a quick technique.

One thing I must add is the need to consider the distance and angle from which the technique is delivered. At close range (grappling distance), circular techniques (e.g., *mawashi uchi* and *mawashi geri*) are very effective as they are not visible and make it easier to create a large impact. At such a short distance, even though it is possible, it is extremely difficult to create such an impact with a *choku zuki* or a *mae geri*.

3.   Smoother Movements

Circular movements may look smoother than linear movements, and a smooth motion is definitely more effective than a jerky one. But, are all linear movements jerky? You might say, "Not necessarily." But, it is true that a linear motion inherently has that tendency. Why so?

Let's look at the motion of a piston. We know that this motion can easily become jerky because it must stop its movement every time it gets to the end of its travel and be pulled back before it can repeat. For this reason, a linear movement inherently has a tendency to become jerky and needs further explanation. In fact, I am sure you agree that it is not too difficult to come to a complete stop with a movement such as what is found in *choku zuki*. You might ask, "Well, then why do you say a piston's motion can easily become jerky?"

To be able to understand the answer to this question, you must first understand the mechanics of tension and relaxation. I know you are familiar with these terms and you believe you control them as you practice your karate. But, I ask, "Can you really?" Believe it or not, achieving complete relaxation is a technique that requires an extremely high level of control over one's body mechanics. Most practitioners try to totally relax their muscles, but they are, in fact, more tense than relaxed.

I am sure you have seen an inexperienced driver on the road who keeps one foot on the brake pedal while pressing the accelerator with the other. This driver is always applying some degree of braking action to his car; thus, it is not running at the speed it would without the additional drag. He also needs more time to stop his car since he is pressing the accelerator as he presses the brake. A similar situation often happens with your muscles during your punches. At the end of a *choku zuki*, the stopping action of your fist is not an instantaneous but rather a sort of dragging motion, and the next movement will be, yes, jerky.

We rarely see a *ren zuki* (連突き) of more than five or six punches in our *kumite* matches, but in a boxing match, we often see combinations of six or more straight punches in one action or exchange. If you remember great boxers such as Muhammad Ali and "Sugar" Ray Leonard, I am sure you will recall that their *ren zuki* were smooth and fast. They never gave the impression of jerkiness, did they?

Now we need to look at some of the drawbacks of circular movements. Yes, we must understand the disadvantages and the unattractive side of circular movements in order to fully appreciate our karate techniques.

1. Longer Distance

I have already mentioned this before, but it is a scientific fact that a straight line is the shortest distance between two points. We all know this. This means that any type of circular route that ties these two points together is longer than a straight one. If their speeds are identical, a circular movement will take longer to reach the target than a straight one. According to this theory, a *choku zuki* to the opponent's head will reach the target sooner than a *mawashi zuki*.

2. Higher Visibility

Another fact is that most circular techniques are structurally more visible. A good example may be that an *uraken uchi* is more visible than a *choku zuki*.

Naturally, the larger a circular movement is, the more visible it will be. Though *mawashi geri* and *mae geri* both use circular movements, the former is definitely more visible as it has a larger circular motion that even includes the hip region. *Mae geri*, on the other hand, has a smaller circular action that is confined to the part of the leg beneath the knee and is thus much less noticeable. This is the major reason *mae geri* is found in many *kata*, but the Okinawan masters did not incorporate *mawashi geri* into any *kata*. Unsu may be an exception, but it can be disputed as I explain in detail in Chapter 4: "Mikazuki Geri, an Extinct Kick?"

A similar tendency is observed in modern-day tournaments. *Mae geri* is less visible and possibly faster, which means it is easier to score with; therefore, *mae geri* is the most popular kicking technique used to score a point. From a martial arts perspective, the issue of visibility is a very serious matter. In a life-or-death situation, you want your technique to be as unnoticeable and stealthy as possible.

So, now how would you answer if I were to ask, "Are circular movements better than linear ones?" Well, I hope you would answer, "Not necessarily."

This is why we need to learn and use both types of techniques. As we all know, it is more advantageous to have different types of weapons in a real battle. In hand-to-hand combat, the concept is still the same. Straight and linear techniques have unique advantages, and circular techniques have their own advantages. In Shotokan karate, we indeed have both kinds of techniques.

Then, why do some of us feel that our karate is linear and jerky? Well, that is the big question, and we must find the answer, but we must know the reasons and causes before we can fix these "problems." I wish to present several facts as causes for these issues. Let me present two causes for the "jerky problem" and one big cause for the "linear look."

First, let's look at the causes for our jerky and rigid movements. One cause is *kime*; the other is tournament *kumite*.

If you are a hard-core Shotokan practitioner, you might burst out, saying, "What's wrong with *kime*? You need *kime* to knock down an opponent. How could it be a major cause?"

As I mentioned before, I have already written about the effects of wrong *kime* in Chapter 1: "Kime" of *Shotokan Myths*. I am not going to explain this with any depth here, so I'll get right to the point. We are too tense and are holding *kime* too long. We were not taught how to relax and generate proper *kime*, so we look like a car with an overly cautious driver who steps on both the accelerator and the brake. We just need to let our foot off the brake, but this is more easily said than done.

To learn how to relax is much more difficult, believe it or not, than to learn how to tense up. Hirokazu Kanazawa (金澤弘和, 1931–) took up tai chi (formerly *tai chi chuan* or *tàijíquán* [太極拳]) to supplement his training so that he could be more relaxed. The late Asai Sensei took *chi gong*, or *kiko* (気功, 'ki training'), to train his body to be more relaxed. It is unfortunately true that out-of-the-box Shotokan karate training does not sufficiently teach us how to relax and pays too much attention to *kime* and tension. As a result, our movements tend to look jerky.

Now we need to see what is involved in tournament *kumite* to understand why this adds to the jerky movements. As we all know, in a *sundome* (寸止め, 'one-inch stop') noncontact tournament, points are given by the referee. His job is to watch the competitors' techniques and award a point if he determines that an attacking technique was effective. If a competitor throws a good technique but hits his opponent and knocks him down, he gets a warning or even loses the match even though the technique was indeed effective.

Competitors must pull or stop their techniques to score a point. Pulling back has become so important that I have heard some practitioners focus their practice more on how to execute a fast *hikite* (引き手, 'drawing hand') than on how to throw a strong punch. Stopping short is not an inherent characteristic of circular techniques; thus, it is rare to see a *shuto uchi* or an *uraken uchi* at a tournament.

Circular techniques are very effective in a close-range fighting situation for two reasons. One is that the angle of a punch or kick is most effective if it lands at ninety degrees, and circular techniques accomplish this at short distances.

The other reason is their invisibility at short distances. I have pointed out that circular techniques are more visible than linear techniques in general. However, in a short-distance situation, a movement coming from the side gets outside the field of vision and is thus less visible.

However, when opponents get within so-called grappling distance, the referee quickly stops the fight and forces them to step back. In addition, a round technique, such as *mawashi uchi* or *kagi zuki*, at such a distance will most likely not be recognized as a scoring technique by the judges. I have experienced this in my own tournament days. The judges would give me a *waza ari* (技有り) for my *choku zuki* and *gyaku zuki*, but when I would deliver a *mawashi zuki*, though it was very strong and fast, I never could score a point with it.

A similar situation exists in the competition *kata* found at tournaments. Since you have to show your movements, you must stop and hold your position for a long time—although it may be just a few seconds, I consider it too long—at several *kime* points. If you run through the movements as a series of combinations, your *kata* will not score high.

However, a true *kata* performance should be done in one stroke, so to speak, with no real stops in the middle. It is like hand-brushed calligraphy of a sentence written in kanji. The brush must make a connection from one kanji to another even

if the stroke is not visible. Sometimes you may see a line of small drops of ink from the end of one kanji to the beginning of the next, which shows that the connection is indeed there.

As long as practitioners participate in tournaments, this trend cannot be avoided. So, what can you do? Well, it all depends on what your purpose is. If you want to win tournaments, then you have to use whatever techniques you need to win. But, if you wish to excel as a martial artist, then you need to go beyond the tournament techniques and practice all the techniques that would work in a real fight. The term *real fight* needs to be defined and further discussed, but I will not do so here in this chapter due to the lack of space. I'll just state that it is a fight without any rules or barred techniques.

Now let's summarize the aspects of Shotokan karate that make our performance look linear, which are our *kata* and *kumite* training.

Let's take a look at our *kata* first. As you will recall, we were talking about the *enbusen*'s being linear. The long *kiba dachi* and exclusively sideways movement of Tekki *kata* make it look extremely linear. By the way, this is a mysterious *kata* in and of itself, and I include two chapters on it in my book *Shotokan Myths*.

The other *kata* have turns (most of them being either 90 or 180 degrees), and some have angled movements, but the lines are still very straight. As we know, in Shotokan *kata*, we have no circular *enbusen* like what we find in *bāguàzhǎng* (八卦掌), a style of kung fu whose *enbusen* are a combination of circular steps and footwork (as shown in the photo at the top of the following page).

For the interested reader, here is an excellent *bāguàzhǎng kata*, Liùshísì Zhǎng (六十四掌, 'Sixty-Four Palms'). Watch the beautiful and smooth performance by an old master here: www.youtube.com/watch?v=c8G2bEzsgHs. As you watch this *kata*, you will quickly notice that the performer simply walks in circles, multiple and complex circles.

In Shotokan, we do not have any *kata* like this one. Asai Sensei recognized this, and I heard that he created a *kata* called *En no Kata* (円の形, 'Circle Form'), but no record of this *kata* is known to exist. He also created Tekki Mugen (鉄騎無限, 'Iron Horse Riding, Infinite'), a modified Tekki form that can be performed in a circular—or almost any other shape, for that matter—*enbusen*. Just imagine! This truly linear *kata*, Tekki, can be performed in a circle, a square, a double loop, etc. I must tell you that it is indeed fun to run Tekki Mugen in different-shaped *enbusen*. Asai Sensei also taught me how to do all of the Heian *kata* in a circle, which is a very creative and interesting *kata* modification.

For those who are interested in a style of Shotokan karate that applies more circular techniques, I suggest you take a look at Asai-style Shotokan karate. In Asai Ryu (浅井流) Shotokan, you need to pay more attention to relaxing before thinking of *kime*. In ASAI, we practice more than thirty Asai *kata*, which supplement the standard JKA *kata*.

If you are interested, you can easily find Asai *kata* such as Suishu, Kashu, Kakuyoku, and Meikyo Nidan on *YouTube* as well as in the *Kata Kyohon* textbooks. As you will see, these *kata* are based on many circular movements. I am sure you will agree that all the techniques you see there flow very nicely, and you

see no jerky motions.

The second aspect of Shotokan karate that makes our performance look linear is our *kumite* syllabus, particularly *sanbon kumite* and *gohon kumite*. In these exercises, the defender is taught to step backward while the opponent steps forward and attacks. It's ingrained into our mind that we naturally step backward when we engage an attacker.

Is this bad? No, it isn't if you are an eighth or seventh *kyu*. Beginners are not ready to learn the more advanced and more appropriate steps (e.g., shifting to the sides, switching feet, or stepping in), so *sanbon* and *gohon kumite* are very good introductory exercises for them. However, the problem is that these exercises are continually used for intermediate and advanced students. This is because they are "fun" and less challenging than *ippon kumite* (if done correctly). So, in many dojo, we witness *sanbon* and *gohon kumite* being used for *kumite* training even for intermediate and advanced students.

This chapter is not about *kumite*, so I will not expand on the idea of how *kumite* training should be conducted here. I will just point out the fact that frequent *sanbon* and *gohon kumite* exercise add to the impression that our training looks linear. We all know that in *jiyu kumite* and in a street fight, complex and irregular shifting patterns emerge.

I am not proposing that *sanbon* and *gohon kumite* be eliminated or banned. I am proposing that more *ippon kumite* and *jiyu ippon kumite* be practiced by intermediate and advanced students with much emphasis on not shifting straight backward. Students must be told that stepping straight backward is the worst option to choose in a fight, which is explained in detail in Chapter 5: "Disparity between Kata and Kumite."

Conclusion

So, in conclusion, let me ask the original question: do we have to introduce more circular techniques into Shotokan? Hopefully, your answer is no. By now, you should also know what we need to do. You will agree that we simply need to use more of the circular techniques we already have. In addition, we need to learn to relax more so that we can make our linear movements smoother and more fluid.

If you look closely at the techniques in our *kata*, provided they are done correctly, you will recognize and appreciate that many of the techniques we find are very circular and beautiful. If you claim you are practicing *budo* karate, then you need to be able to apply these techniques to your *kumite*. Once this is mastered, you will have a harmonious combination of linear and circular techniques that is surprisingly effective in real fighting.

押忍

CHAPTER EIGHT
第八章

STRAIGHT TECHNIQUES WITHIN CIRCULAR MOVEMENTS
円運動による直線技の謎

I know you are confused about the title of this chapter. I do not blame you if you are confused as it does not make sense to have a straight technique in anything circular. Straight and circular do not match or accommodate each other, or at least this seems to be the case.

Let me explain. The title of the last chapter was "Does Shotokan Lack Circular Techniques?" The conclusion was that we need to use more of the circular techniques we already have. I also pointed out that we need to learn to relax more so that we can make our linear movements smoother and more fluid. In that chapter, I omitted an important factor: how to merge circular movements into linear techniques. I would like to attempt to describe this unusual concept in this chapter.

I have mentioned that many Shotokan practitioners look stiff and awkward. Their linear and square moves come from unnatural movements, which are the result of excessive tension. This is sadly true. But, if you observe real experts, Shotokan instructors such as Asai, Yahara, Osaka, and Kanazawa, this is not the case. Their performances show no stiffness or excessive tension even in their linear techniques.

Does this come only from relaxing more? Proper relaxation is definitely key, but there are a couple of other important factors they use that we must know. I am happy to share these ideas with the reader, but first let us review the circular techniques we have in Shotokan. I listed many circular techniques with illustrations in the last chapter. Let us review those circular techniques first, and then I will provide and example for each category.

Keri Waza (蹴り技, 'Kicking Techniques')

Mawashi geri is a great example of a kick that requires circular movement of

the kicking leg. So is *yoko geri keage*. Even a straight-looking *mae geri* is delivered with a pendulum-like swing of the part of the leg between the knee and the foot.

Mawashi geri is such a popular example of a circular technique. Let's find out if it can be executed as a straight technique.

We are taught to bring our knee up to the side by ninety degrees or more. First of all, this requires a lot of balancing practice, and I recommend that all of us spend much time training in this exercise. This particular exercise is not really for flexibility. Rather, it is for strengthening the side and back muscles

that are necessary not only for *mawashi geri* but also for *yoko geri* and *ushiro geri*. But, bringing the knee this high is only for *kihon* training, particularly for *kyu* students. When you get to be a *dan* student, this is not how you should prepare for *mawashi geri* in a *kumite* situation.

How are we supposed to do it, then? You may be surprised or may not like what you find, but you lift the knee forward as you do in *mae geri*. With the leg tightly tucked, you bring the knee straight up toward the opponent, and, at the last moment, you quickly rotate your hips and throw the kicking foot in a small circular motion to the opponent's temple or *jodan*.

This kick is called *mikazuki geri* in Kyokushinkai (極真会), which is a full-contact style. However, most Shotokan dojo do not teach it. In fact, the instructors will tell you to bring the knee up to the side. When I was competing in the seventies and eighties, you could not score with this kick. As I am not currently very active in tournament judging, I do not know whether or not this trend has changed in the last twenty years or so.

We can talk about *yoko geri*, but, believe it or not, the delivery concept for this kick is the same as in *mawashi geri* or *mikazuki geri*. In other words, you execute *yoko geri* as you would *mae geri* until the last moment.

In *kata*, though many different stances are used, the kick itself is thrown most-ly sideways (e.g., Heian Nidan, Heian Yondan, Kanku, etc.). Only in Sochin is it done to the rear, which is one of the more challenging techniques in this *kata*. In *kihon* training, you are probably taught to execute *yoko geri* from *kiba dachi*.

Bruce Lee (李小龍, 1940–1973) was a famous ac-tor, and it is amazing how popular he still is even though he died over forty years ago. He definitely was a much better actor than martial artist. I give him a lot of credit for making Asian martial arts popular through his kung fu movies. Anyway, he used *yoko geri kekomi* from *kiba dachi* in his movies, so a lot of people have tried to imi-tate this.

It is very interesting that Bruce Lee favored this method as this move is so straight and linear, whereas he was always preaching circular techniques. Unlike his Wing Chun (詠春) master, the late Ip Man (葉問, 1893–1972), Lee adopted a wide *kiba dachi* in his movies. Ip Man, on the other hand, used a short, natural stance for his short-distance Wing Chun techniques.

I can understand why Lee used *kiba dachi* as it is more visually appealing on the big screen. So was the sidestepping move he used with *yoko geri kekomi*, which would hurl his opponent into the air, showing the tremendous power that his kick had supposedly generated. This is why I say that Lee was a very visual person. He knew exactly how he would appear on the big screen, and that is precisely why he was so successful in his movies. Kung fu action sequences are very popular in movies now, so the moves from those old movies are no longer unique. But, they were in the seventies, when Lee brought about a revolution in action movies.

I used to see a fighting style in the seventies and eighties that imitated Lee's style. In current tournaments, I witness a lot of hopping by *kumite* competitors, and this may be a holdover from Lee's heritage. The debate over *kiba dachi* and hopping, though interesting, is not the topic at hand, so I will not go into this here, but I will touch on this subject again in Chapter 10: "Gravity, Friend or Foe?"

For the most effective *yoko geri*, whether *keage* or *kekomi*, you need to assume either a full or half *zenkutsu dachi* and kick using the rear leg. Executing *yoko geri* to the front from *zenkutsu dachi* is challenging, but it can be done smoothly if you raise your knee up just as you would with *mae geri*. At the last moment, you quickly rotate your hips ninety degrees (much more than you would with *mawashi geri*) and execute *yoko geri*.

There are a couple of important things that need to accompany this kick. One is the need to minimize arm movement. This is the same for all kicks as movement of the arms is a telltale sign to the opponent that you are going to kick. You need to separate your upper-body movements from those of your lower body. In other words, the arms must not be used to generate hip rotation. This concept may be the complete opposite of what you were taught or have learned.

You minimize arm movement, but to balance out the rotation of the hips, you reverse rotate only the shoulders, which means your upper body faces forward the entire time. This is not a difficult concept, but executing it is hard and requires intense training. Though the shoulders are reverse rotated, the hands must show minimal movement. They should be kept up high so that they can be used for *jodan* protection and a follow-up punch.

The second important thing is the need for a quick reverse hip rotation after the kick, which causes the hips to face forward and allows you to land in a full or half *zenkutsu dachi*. It is easier to land with the hips sideways in *kiba dachi*, and though this is an option while you are learning how to execute *yoko geri* toward the front from *zenkutsu dachi*, you must avoid this in *kumite*. In *kumite*, your feet and hips should always be facing the opponent except during the execution of some techniques.

I wish I could explain this mechanism better, but doing so with words is extremely difficult. If you do not understand these finer points, I apologize for my poor ability to explain. It would be much easier for me to use my body to explain them in person. I am a main contributor to Karate Coaching's online instruction service (www.karatecoaching.com), and I create many instructional videos there. The fee is very reasonable, and the content is educational for all levels of Shotokan practitioners. I invite the reader to subscribe to this service.

Uke Waza (受け技, 'Blocking Techniques')

This concept is also very visible in the blocking techniques. The obvious one is *soto ude uke*, in which the blocking arm is swung very widely in a circular movement as the block is thrown. Even in a less obvious blocking technique, such as *age uke* or *gedan barai*, a circular movement of the blocking arm is used.

How do you execute *soto ude uke*? You bring your blocking arm up just as you do in *shuto uchi*. In other words, you are taught to bring the blocking hand high and behind your head before starting the circular motion of *ude uke*.

Then, how do you throw a straight *soto ude uke*? Assume a natural stance as you would in *ippon kumite*. As you step backward or forward to throw your block, you do not bring your blocking arm high and back. Instead, you bring your arm to the front as though you would touch the opponent's punching arm. When the opponent's fist is near your *chudan* or *jodan* target, you quickly pull back your blocking arm by dropping the elbow down and rotating the wrist. You do not even need to move your arm sideways to block the punch as you will rotate your hips and upper body slightly, which will give the sideways motion that is necessary to block the punch.

This action is smooth and very fast. It also makes what you are trying to do less obvious to the opponent. You may say, "Hey, isn't that cheating?" My answer is no. Of course, this is not what you will teach a white belt or even a brown belt, but this is what you need to do in *jiyu kumite* and in a real fight.

Tsuki Kogeki Waza (突き攻撃技, 'Attacking Hand Techniques')

How about the attacking techniques that use our arms? A very obvious technique is *shuto uchi*, in which the open hand is used in a very circular manner. Another good example is *uraken uchi*. Here the fist is delivered with a very circular movement of the arm.

As an example of this category, I will pick *shuto uchi*, which we find in Heian Yondan and Kanku Dai. We are taught to bring the striking arm up behind our head and extend the elbow to the side before executing the circular rotation of the *shuto*. Yes, this is a textbook movement, and this is how we should learn it when we are *kyu* students. To get maximum speed by minimizing distance, however, you do not bring your striking arm as high, and you do not pull back.

It is hard to describe this with words, but the striking arm is shot almost straight up from the *shizentai* position (arms dangling in front of you). The striking hand is shot to the outside of the target area, such as the neck or temple. When the hand reaches maximum distance (hopefully right next to the target area), you pull it back suddenly as you would do with a whip when you want to crack it. As the hand returns, it makes a slight circular motion toward the target and strikes it. This is the point at which a whip would make a cracking sound. If this is done correctly, it will be very invisible and also very fast.

OK, I am sure the reader will agree that these techniques are performed with vivid circular movements. I would like to bring up the not-so-well-known fact that circular techniques were discouraged or disliked by the ancient masters on Okinawa. If you are a *budo karateka*, you can figure out why this was the case.

There are some downsides to circular techniques. The biggest shortcoming for the martial artist is that these techniques are very visible to the opponent because of the circular paths they travel. This is a big no-no if you are fighting for your life.

The second drawback is the simple mathematical fact that a circular path is longer than a straight one, which means it usually takes more time to get to the end point. This assertion is based on the assumption that the speed of the techniques is the same. If the speed of a circular technique is faster than that of a straight technique, then it could take the same or less time to reach the target. However, this does not normally happen, so we can say that a straight technique, such as *choku zuki*, is faster than a circular technique, such as *shuto uchi* or *uraken uchi*.

At the same time, this fact may not mean much in a free-for-all fight as other factors are just as or more important than the simple speed of the technique. Other important factors are distance, timing, rhythm, accuracy, power, appropriateness of the technique, etc.

Despite the shortcomings of circular techniques, these masters used them. How did they do this? You may be surprised to hear a simple answer, but they simply minimized the circular nature of their techniques. Really? Yes, they did this to minimize visibility and distance. This is done not only in strikes but also in kicks and blocks, as discussed in the previous sections.

So, I have described how the experts make their circular techniques smaller so that they become closer to straight or linear techniques. I have also explained two major reasons they do this. Despite the fact that they endeavor to make all their techniques linear and straight, they do not look stiff or rigid.

Of course, they are more relaxed, and their techniques look smooth, but there is one other major factor that makes their movements less linear and more fluid. It is that their hip rotation includes *tai sabaki* and *tenshin*.

Taisabaki (体裁き) is body shifting, and *tenshin* (転身) is body rotation. Both techniques are used for dodging or averting the opponent's attacks. They not only dodge or avert but also put the defender into a better position to counterattack.

The late Asai Sensei was a true expert at *taisabaki* and *tenshin*, which involved numerous kinds of rotations, including a 360-degree turn. He would execute the blocks and counterattacks as he rotated. By the time the rotation was complete, the *kumite* had already been finished.

You cannot appreciate this performance as much as you can once you have seen it from a bird's-eye view on a video recorded by a camera set on the ceiling. The movements of the rotation are very smooth, and it almost looks like a video of a dance. Asai Sensei's movements especially do not only go in circles; his body waves and ducks. He sinks underneath a kick or a punch and then reappears standing right behind the attacker. During the body shifting and rotation, he is blocking and counterattacking at the same time.

The movements are all in one motion with a beautiful flow of different speeds and tempos. They are somewhat like the waves of the ocean yet different as they are totally unpredictable. His moves are all natural, and there is no break between them. One technique is smoothly connected to the next and then on to the next until the opponent is totally devastated. I think this is where the beauty appears and is unlike the artificial circular movements of a dancer.

There is a different level of beauty that comes from the ability of an expert who is able to create flowing movements in unrehearsed actions. To be able to do this, your movements must be not only relaxed but also fluid. They must be complex and sophisticated as well as precise and free. At least one Shotokan master, a karate genius, left us a perfect example that we can follow if we wish to acquire and master the fluid and circular motions within the linear techniques of Shotokan karate.

押忍

CHAPTER NINE
第九章

UNSTABLE BALANCE
不安定な安定の謎

What would you say if I told you that good balance is bad for karate? You would probably protest and say, "Bull!" If you think I'm joking, I am sorry but I'm very serious about this. I will explain what I mean as many practitioners, including the senior ones, do not understand this.

First, you may say, "Wait a minute. We practice a low *kiba dachi* to strengthen our legs. We learn how to keep good balance. Are you now trying to tell us that good balance is bad?" Yes, I understand what you are saying, and you are right. We need to have strong legs and good stances.

I can almost hear you saying, "Now you are telling us that good stances are important. Then, good balance is a good thing, isn't it?" My answer to you is yes and no. I know you are confused now. Let me explain. I say yes because we are very unique among the mammal species in the way we stand. Specifically, we are the only mammal that stands on two legs. We do not stand like a dog or a horse.

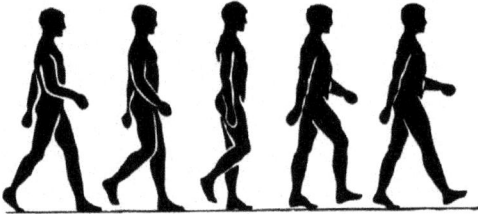

You may say, "We all know that, but why you are making a big deal about this?" I understand why you ask this question, but this is exactly why I am making a big deal about it. We, all of us, do not recognize the true uniqueness of the bipedal ability we gained as we developed ourselves as *Homines sapientes* hundreds of thousands of years ago.

We all know that a baby does not learn how to walk from the very beginning. It has to go through a stage of crawling. In other words, it needs to walk on its hands and feet like a dog or a horse. Conveniently, its legs are proportionately much shorter, so crawling is an easier task than it would be if an adult were to attempt it.

We watch a baby about a year old who tries so hard to walk. First, you hold out your hands and help him. Then, eventually, you let his hands go for a second or two. The baby balances on his own for a second and then sits down. This process goes on for a few days, but he will eventually learn how to take one step forward at first. Then, it's two, three, etc.

Before the baby gets to this stage, he crawls, and he can move pretty quickly. Obviously, four legs give us much better balance and require less skill to keep that balance. But, we do not remember having learned this as we were only one year old.

On the other hand, you may remember when you were a toddler or when you learned how to ride a bike. Initially, your bike had training wheels, right? The two extra wheels gave the bike a total of four wheels. You needed to spend some painful time falling off many times. But, in the end, you learned how to ride a bike on two wheels, which is the special and challenging skill of gaining balance.

Anyway, walking on two legs is a mysterious thing, and even scholars have different opinions as to why *Homo sapiens* chose to stand up when he branched off from the forefather species. As this is not a chapter on human evolution, we will skip the discussion on this particular point. But, the importance of this unique walking mechanism must be recognized.

As I mentioned earlier, we learn how to walk in our first year of life, and then we forget the process. When we try to remember our first days, we recall having always been able to walk. This is why we do not want to believe that we are not well balanced or that balancing is an issue when we walk. In fact, it is true for most of us that keeping balance as we walk is not an issue.

I challenge you to think this over again. Are we really well balanced on only two legs? People think it is funny when we slip on a banana peel, but why? Be-

cause we all of a sudden realize that we are not well balanced. If you have learned how to skate or ski, do you remember how you were on your first lesson or the day you stepped onto a skating rink for the first time? I do, and I remember clearly how off-balance I was. I had to hang on to the wall of the ice skating rink. No one can skate well from the very beginning. You have to learn how to keep your balance before you learn how to skate or ski. I remember that I had to hold on to the wall like a baby who was trying to learn how to walk.

Let's look at another example. When you need to have good balance in a wrestling match, you naturally get down on your hands and knees or hands and feet. This is the most balanced position you can assume.

This concept is the same in the martial arts. In judo, they teach you to get into a stance called *jigotai* (自護体), which is shown in the historic photo of Jigoro Kano to the left (Kano is the one on the right). Here the *judoka* does not get down on his hands and knees, but he gets the same effect by holding on to his opponent. Using the legs of the opponent, the *judoka* achieves a four-legged stance, which is the most balanced stance.

Balance is also important for the *karateka*. This is why we practice a low stance such as *kiba dachi* for a long time to strengthen our legs. Many readers can probably remember a training session in which your sensei kept you standing in *kiba dachi* for thirty minutes or more. Maybe some readers have had to

carry a fellow *karateka* on their shoulders. Yes, all those tough exercises are to strengthen the legs so that you will have good balance in your stances.

The most popular stance in Shotokan is definitely *zenkutsu dachi*, the front stance. Your sensei will tell you to put your feet at shoulder width, which is important as you will have a problem with balance if your feet are too narrow. In addition, your sensei will tell you to bend your front knee so that you will have a low stance. Here again, this low stance is required.

Stances, *tachikata* (立ち方) in Japanese, are the foundation of karate techniques. The stronger the legs are, the better the balance can be. My sensei gave me an analogy of the stance as being the base of a cannon and the punch as being the cannon itself. If our stance is weak, then the cannon base is a rowboat. Can you imagine what would happen if you shot a cannon from a small rowboat? If your stance is strong and solid, this is like having a tank as a base. Speaking of tanks, this reminds me of the late Keinosuke Enoeda (榎枝慶之輔, 1935–2003), whose nickname in Japan was *Tank* because of his powerful technique, which was based on the solid foundation of his stance (photo left).

OK, I am sure you will agree with all that I have described so far. All I have written about is how important good balance is for karate. You already knew all this and might say that I am wasting your time. Hopefully, I am not wasting your time, and you will see this as you read further. You may also tell me that it is ridiculous to claim that good balance is bad. I am trying to prove to you that my claim is not that ridiculous. Now, give me a chance and let me explain why I say that good balance is bad.

OK, let me ask you something. Is karate made up of dead stops? The picture above shows the final phase of *gyaku zuki*. Despite how great the technique may have been, it is finished and done with. What I am trying to say is that karate techniques are dynamic. Too much importance is ascribed to the end product, but it is the process that is actually more important. In other words, no matter how fast and strong that *gyaku zuki* may be, if the practitioner fails to deliver it to the target, it has no meaning and has not accomplish its most important task, which is punching the opponent.

I can hear you say, "We know this. This is why we not only practice in position but also practice a lot of *kihon*." (The correct Japanese term is actually *ido geiko* [移動稽古]. *Ido* [移動] means 'shifting' or 'movement', and *keiko/-geiko* [稽古] means 'training' or 'practice'.) As far as I know, no instructors teach students, particularly senior students, to stay off-balance. You might ask, "Did you say, 'stay off-balance'?" My answer is yes. It may sound crazy, but we overemphasize good balance. On the other hand, we miss or ignore another extremely important requirement in our karate techniques: being off-balance. Yes, you are now asking, "What do you mean by that?" So, let me explain.

Let's look at a good example. If you are a brown belt or above, then you must know the popular *kihon kata* Bassai Dai. The *kamae* for this *kata* is shown in the photo to the left. OK, when you assume this *kamae*, what does your sensei tell you to do? He commands you to take a quick step or jump forward and execute a strong *uraken uchi*, right? If so, then does he teach you how to do this?

In other words, you are in *heisoku dachi*, and to take a quick step or jump will require a special technique. Unfortunately, most instructors do not or cannot teach you how to do this. Some may tell you to push off the ground with your left foot. If you are lucky, some will tell you to bring your right knee up and forward when you want to jump forward. And, if you are really lucky and have an excellent instructor, he will tell you to lean slightly forward like the Leaning Tower of Pisa in Italy. Though this is not exactly the correct posture, he is telling you the right thing. I will explain exactly how you should position your body for this *kamae* later, but, for now, let me continue with my explanation of the importance of instability, i.e., being off-balance.

Let me bring up another analogy along with a visual example to explain what I am trying to say. Just think about holding a stick or a *bo*. The easiest way to keep the stick upright is to grab it firmly with your hand (Figure 1), but you can also balance it on your palm (Figure 2).

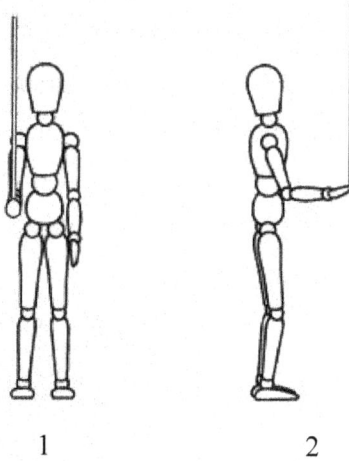

1   2

Doing this will require a balancing technique. So, what I am saying is that most of us are standing like Figure 1, while the baby is walking more or less like Figure 2. You may say, "OK, so what? Is this a problem?" This is a very daring thing to say, and I risk the possibility of being misunderstood, but my answer is yes, and here is the core of the point I am trying to make. The ability to stand firm, as in Figure 1, is precisely the problem for all *karateka*. We must maintain the ability to keep balance, as in Figure 2.

So, you may say, "I don't understand how being able to stand firm is a problem. Are you are saying we need to walk like a baby?" My answer is yes and no. Are you totally confused now? Let me continue with my explanation. The ability to stand firm is good in and of itself, but we are holding the stick too hard. What I am saying is that most of us are overusing our muscles just to stand up or overcompensating with our muscles when we stand, walk, or run. I am not talking about just the legs but also the hips, back, torso, and neck, which means most of your body muscles.

You may not believe this, but it is true. Ask yourself if you can stand up for hours without getting tired. If your body is totally relaxed while you stand up, you can do it. However, most of us will get tired because a lot of unnecessary muscles are being used, and even the necessary muscles are being overtightened or used more than necessary.

So, what is wrong with that? Nothing because all you need to do is sit down when you get tried. However, if you are a serious karate practitioner or athlete, this subject is very important. Then, how is it wrong if you are overly tense or are using unnecessary muscles? Let's take a look at a couple of the best examples. Though Michael Jordan and Pelé retired many years ago, we still remember them as two of the greatest basketball and soccer players.

Jordan, also known as *Air Jordan,* had a long and impressive jump shot, but I was more impressed with his ability to duck and weave through the defensive players of the opposing team. These players were all professional athletes, and they were the best defenders, but Jordan wove through them so easily that it was as though they did not even see him. By the way, he used to stick his tongue out as he dribbled through the defense (as shown in the photo above). There is a good reason for this. I am not sure if it has been discussed by anyone before, but this action and his ability to balance are connected. This may be an interesting subject for a future discussion.

Pelé was the same. His kicks in the air were impressive, but his magic was his ability to weave through his opponents as though they were not there to defend.

How were these two able do this? They

were talented, yes, but the secret was that both of them were totally relaxed and knew how to lose their balance in order to make those explosive moves. It is true that they were ball players and not karate practitioners. But, look at masters such as Asai, Enoeda, Kanazawa, Okazaki, and others. They were all flexible, and I am not talking about just in their hip joints but in all other key joints, such as in their shoulders. In addition, their muscles were all relaxed, and I have not known any one of them to be stiff.

So, now you will agree that we must be relaxed and not stiff, but you will ask why we have to be off-balance for karate. The simple answer is that karate is dynamic. In other words, we need to be able to move very quickly. In a basketball or football play, you need to go around the defender, but in karate, though the principle of the moves is the same, you need to get your *waza* (whether a punch or a kick) to the opponent before he can evade or block it. You must have gravitational pull to initiate your move.

But, you may argue, saying, "I have a set of strong legs, so I can push the ground with my rear foot and move forward very quickly. Why do I need gravitational pull?" This becomes very technical, but if you are interested in *budo* karate, then you need to read on.

When you depend on your rear foot or leg to initiate your move, there is always a movement called *okori* (起こり), which is the Japanese word that refers to a telltale movement. On the other hand, if you "fall," which is exactly what happens when you lose your balance, there is no *okori*; thus, the opponent cannot detect your initial move. Of course, after the initial move, you use your leg muscles and a slight kickoff with your rear foot, but the difference you can make during the first hundredth of a second is so critical in a life-or-death match.

This may mean nothing to you if you are not interested in life-or-death-type fighting or *budo* karate. This also means very little even in a *kumite* match. Why? It is simply because the deciding factor in determining who scores or wins is not the person's punch or kick but rather a third party: the eyes and/or imagination of the judge. The real winner is never known in a tournament. Yes, I am aware that my comment is very controversial and not liked by many, but it does not matter as it cannot be proven wrong.

Well, am I then saying that we need to walk like a baby? No, that is not what I am suggesting. What I am suggesting is that we need to learn to know how to be on the tipping point between balanced and unbalanced. In fact, we need to be familiar with the tipping point where this delicate balance is kept. It is a state of being balanced yet almost losing balance. And, this is the state of being that we need to create when we assume the *kamae* of Bassai Dai.

Yes, in order to take that explosive first step, you need to adopt this state of being almost off-balance in your *kamae*. So, most practitioners lean forward like the Leaning Tower of Pisa. However, this is not what you want to do as it will be too visible to the opponent. The Leaning Tower of Pisa cannot bend in the middle, so it has no choice, but you do. You can keep your upper body vertical while bringing your body forward like the Leaning Tower of Pisa.

How do you do this? You bend your ankle, knee, and hip joints so that your upper body is slightly forward of the center of gravity while still remaining upright. You will get the Leaning Tower of Pisa effect without leaning forward. The important thing is that you not push yourself to the point at which you need to lift your heels up, which is too far. You must be able to keep your heels lightly on the ground but almost coming off of it, which is the perfect state. By pushing your hips slightly forward, you will reach the point at which you are barely keeping your balance. This is the state I call *unstably balanced*, which is what you need to create in your Bassai Dai *kamae*.

So, do we just fall when we start this *kata*, then? Or, do we kick the ground with our feet? My answer is no to both questions. There is an incredible mechanism I will share with you, which not too many instructors teach their students.

The mechanism is quite simple. All you need to do is collapse the knees. Just imagine that you have a pin that is keeping your knees together and your legs upright. To take the initial quick step forward, you imagine that you pull this pin out of your knees with a quick action. Your body will fall downward but slightly forward as you have pushed your hips forward. With this movement, you will achieve forward acceleration faster, believe it or not, than you would by pushing off with your feet or by bringing one leg up as I have seen some practitioners do.

The greatest benefit, however, is not the increase in speed. This is the amazing part of the wisdom of the creator of this *kata*, which, unfortunately, seems to have been lost or nearly lost. The movement you create by shifting your hips forward and falling downward to initiate the first move is very natural and much less detectable by the opponent.

I cannot stress the importance of this subject enough as modern karate has lost interest in the art of invisible or stealth moves. In our regular *kumite* exercises, and even in *kumite* tournaments, this subject is rarely spoken of or considered to be important. Why? It is obviously because *kumite* practitioners expect the opponent to strike with either a punch or a kick.

On the other hand, in a real fighting situation, a wise and well-trained practitioner must give the impression that he is not planning or preparing himself for a first strike. In other words, you want your opponent to believe that you are not going to attack; thus, he will be somewhat less cautious and more off guard.

By acquiring this technique, you will be in a position to use *taisabaki* to move sideways (learned from Tekki) and forward (learned from Bassai Dai) to dodge attacks or to move forward to strike or counterattack. Your body will be like a stick resting on the palm of a hand. In other words, when you are in a conflict or fighting situation, you will not be standing firm like a tree; you will be swaying somewhat, depending on the position and attitude of the opponent. You will continuously shift to the position that

best fits the ever-changing situation of the opponents and environment surrounding you. You will be well prepared to move quickly in any direction by keeping your body unstable and unstably balanced. If you are a tree, you cannot move as it takes a lot of time and energy to move a tree from one spot to another.

As we often witness in *jiyu kumite*, the movements and actions of the *karateka* are continuous, and many techniques are exchanged. This goes on continuously for two minutes or for whatever amount of time the rules allow.

I hate to say this, but it is the same in movie scenes involving street fights or bar fights. This can also be seen in Hong Kong kung fu movies, including the ones with the famous Bruce Lee, in which the actors continue to jump up and fight even after getting hit and punched many times in the face. Movies cannot adopt real fight scenes, which go from total stillness to complete knockout by a quick, undetectable action in just one second.

By the way, one of the kung fu styles that is very interesting is the Drunken Monkey style. You might have seen Jackie Chan (成龍, 1954–) play a comical role (photo left) in one of these movies, *The Forbidden Kingdom* (功夫之王 [Lionsgate, The Weinstein Company, 2008]). By pretending to be drunk, a practitioner of this style is trying to get his opponent to put his guard down, but that is not the only purpose. As you have read what I have written up to this point, you can easily figure out that this drunken style is exactly the unstable balance that surprises the opponent. How wise this style is! I am very impressed with the wisdom the ancient masters possessed.

So, I must say that a real fight is not much fun to watch. In fact, an untrained person will not even see what has happened in front of him. An eyewitness will see the *budo* karate expert move just a little. He will then see the opponent on the ground and not understand how it happened. This is not an exaggeration or a fairy tale. By attaining unstable balance, an expert can move invisibly or in a very unnoticeable way.

Whether you believe this or not does not matter as you can experiment your-self and prove whether what I am saying is true or not. Practice Tekki Shodan to keep the pelvis joints flexible, which enables you to shift sideways very quickly. Practice the first move in Bassai Dai and Bassai Sho, using the method in which the body falls forward, to learn how to shift forward quickly. By combining these two exercises, you can learn to shift almost 360 degrees without any unnecessary effort as well as eliminate any movements of the upper body that would be a tell-tale giveaway.

You may or may not know that we are always unconsciously balancing and counterbalancing as we stand still, which can be seen with a very close exami-nation of the body. Standing still is a result of our successfully managing and controlling the many different muscles of our entire body. We may be under the impression that our body is totally still, perfectly balanced, and thus not moving, but this is far from the truth. It is actually undergoing the continuous balancing and counterbalancing of all the muscles involved.

In fact, professional dancers are aware of this and adopt this concept in their performance. The major ob-jective of dancers is to make their performance beautiful by making their moves smooth and natural. They prac-tice hours to learn how to stand not only on two legs but also on one, and they try hard to avoid looking stiff. They know that they can move smoothly and beautifully only from being balanced in a state of instability.

I believe we can learn a lot from this. Even though dancers are simply trying to have beautiful moves, shouldn't it also be our aim to be able to move smoothly and naturally? I suggest that you test this concept of unstable balance in your training menu. I am sure you will discover a surprising ease of body movement when you discover true balance in a state of instability.

押忍

CHAPTER TEN
第十章

GRAVITY, FRIEND OR FOE?
重力は敵かそれとも味方か？

Have you ever considered the concept of gravitational force in your karate practice? I assume most readers have not added the gravity factor into their training. Many probably disregard it as having nothing to do with their karate training, and even after hearing that gravity is important, they probably still assess its effect as being minuscule.

This is only correct if you do not wish to reach a higher level of karate movement and skill. If you are satisfied with staying at a good *shodan* level, you do not need to consider the concept I present to you here. However, if your interest lies in reaching a higher level, I can tell you that discovering the often-ignored facts about gravitational force will help you. In fact, ignorance of these facts will make gravitational force your enemy. Unfortunately, for many practitioners, this is the sad truth.

Gravitational force is called *gravity* or *gravitation*, and this universal force is what gives weight to objects. Because of gravity, we cannot fly like Superman, even if we try very hard to jump high. It is a natural phenomenon, and all of us are being affected by it all the time. No matter where you go on Earth, you cannot get away from this natural phenomenon. We all know this very well; however, in our daily lives, we just do not recognize this force or weight as it feels so normal to us. If you happened to be on the moon, then the gravity you would experience would be much less (83.3% less to be exact). You would feel much lighter and would be able to jump like a grasshopper. In fact, this has been demonstrated by astronauts who have landed on the moon.

We do not normally notice gravity in our daily lives because we are so adjusted to the feeling of what is happening to our body. Our body weight ties us down to Earth because of gravity. Even when we lift a heavy bag, we do not say, "Boy, gravity is making this bag heavy." We simply think that the bag is heavy.

Few people can run a hundred meters in less than ten seconds, but we never think that gravity is what is preventing us from doing so. We blame our legs for not being strong enough to run that fast. The same can be said of our *kumite* exercise. We wish we could move a bit faster, but we do not blame gravity for preventing us from moving faster or for slowing us down.

OK, enough has been said about how gravitational force is there and how we should recognize it. So what? How does this recognition help? It helps us to realize that gravity can be our enemy, which can lead to improvement.

We recognize that gravity is a universal law of physics, so we might believe there is nothing we can do about this. We cannot reduce gravity, so some may suggest that we reduce our weight. Yes, this idea would work, and I also recommend that those who are overweight go on a diet. Others may suggest that we strengthen our legs, and it may be true that if we had legs like those of Usain Bolt (1986–), we could run faster. Should we, then, be on the leg machine instead of practicing *kata*? Indeed, many do this, but it is not my recommendation. I emphatically state that having legs like Usain Bolt will not help us much in karate (sorry, Usain).

OK, what do we need to move faster, then? Now, this is where it can be tricky. The answer is that we need to leverage gravity. You may say, "You said that gravity was the enemy. Now you are saying we need to use the enemy to improve our speed?" That's right, and we must learn to leverage or use gravity to our advantage.

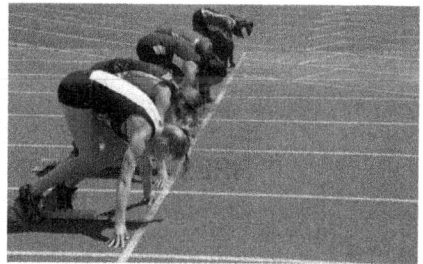

For many practitioners, gravity is working against them. I already mentioned obesity. If you are overweight, you will move more slowly than if you were lighter. This is true, and staying light is a requirement for all karate practitioners, regardless of age. But, even if you are in shape, and your weight is in line, you will still move more slowly if you do not use gravity to your advantage.

Let me elaborate by using Usain Bolt, the fastest man on Earth. When he starts

his hundred-meter dash, how does he stand? Since he is so fast, does he just stand casually at the start of the race? No, he does not stand straight up but instead crouches down and leans his head forward and down with his hips raised high. Why does he do this? Because this is the most effective method for shifting his body from a speed of zero (standing still) to his maximum speed so that he can run a hundred meters in less than ten seconds.

The most important point in this mechanism is that the runner essentially needs to fall forward. The key word here is *fall*. He does this by positioning the heaviest body part, his head, very far forward and downward. If he were to pick up his supporting hands without jumping forward, he would surely fall flat on his face. In order to avoid this, he takes quick steps forward, and these movements translate into a quick acceleration of his body.

Of course, the runner is not simply falling forward. He pushes off the starting blocks with his feet and uses his leg muscles to dash forward. This starting method is universal as it has been proven to produce the quickest start. Once the start occurs, the runner will bring his

head more upright to continue his run. To run faster, we normally just think of our legs and try to take quicker steps. In other words, we believe the key to increasing speed is increasing pace. We rarely think of leaning our upper body forward to increase running speed.

Anyway, this chapter is not meant to be a discussion on the mechanics of running (though it is a very interesting subject). However, I have written about it here because the principle of body shifting in both karate and short-distance running is based on the same concept. The objectives of these two athletic activities, on the other hand, are quite different. The idea of running is to carry the body over a long distance (e.g., a hundred meters) to a goal in the fastest way possible. In karate, however, the distance you need to cover in most situations is probably less than two meters.

If the distance happens to be greater than that, then the karate practitioner simply waits until the opponent moves within critical *maai*. This refers to a distance from which either opponent can strike with one step or one move. I am sure I do not need to go into this particular subject in depth as most readers understand the meaning of critical *maai* and its concept.

What is required for the *karateka* is the ability to move a short distance (less than two meters) in a very quick way. Of course, there are other requirements for his body shifting, and one of them is invisibility. His moves must be as invisible as possible, or his initial motion must not be detected by his opponent. This is a very important point in martial arts, but it has not been fully recognized or appreciated mainly because of the popularity of tournament *kumite*.

In tournament *kumite*, both competitors know each other's intention, so stealth moves have little value in this situation. In a real fight, however, this ability is critical, and it almost always determines who wins. These moves are highly complex and sophisticated. Indeed, these requirements are very challenging and difficult to master, and this necessitates a certain technique and special training.

In the previous chapter, I wrote on how to keep one's balance in a state of instability. As I explained in that chapter, you need to shift your center of gravity so that you will be balanced in a state instability, which is a state in which you will fall if someone gives you a little tap on the shoulder. Without revealing it to your opponent, you are leaning like the Leaning Tower of Pisa.

Another analogy is the water that is held by a dam. Water collected at a high elevation has a hidden energy. When the water rushes out through the gate, this energy is used to turn a turbine and create electrical power. So, to move quickly, you need to leverage gravity. This is extremely important as not too many instructors are aware of or appreciate this fact.

The ability to move quickly is not the only benefit we can get from grav-

ity. There is another key benefit. The picture to the left is a very famous one (at least in Japan). Pictured here are Kenwa Mabuni, the founder of Shito Ryu, and his son, who is leaning against him. This picture illustrates the power of *tokiho* (倒木法), which literally means 'method or rule of falling wood' and states that once gravitational force is behind a light person, a bigger and stronger person will have a problem sustaining his position or pushing the light person back without the need for the latter to apply any additional force.

So, you say, "OK, so what? Karate is kicks and punches. This method may be good for judo or jujutsu, but how does it affect my karate techniques?" I understand why you would ask this question as this subject is not normally taught or even mentioned in the average karate lesson or dojo.

After learning the basic stances and *sonoba geiko* (その場稽古, 'in-position practice'), you learn *ido geiko* (移動稽古, 'shifting practice'). The first thing you learn in *ido geiko* is probably the stepping punch, an illustration of which is shown to the right.

After a while, your sensei gets you into *kumite*, and the first *kumite* you learn is either *sanbon kumite* or *gohon kumite*. What you discover here is that your *senpai* (先輩, 'senior students') easily block your punches. Yes, they are your seniors, so they are faster. You may not question this, but you feel that your punches are not that powerful. When you execute a counterattack with your *gyaku zuki*, you are not certain you could honestly knock out an opponent with that punch if you really wanted to.

So, you put more power into your punches, and your sensei tells you to relax. *What shall I do next?* you wonder. Then, you discover the *makiwara* (巻藁), a great karate invention that I wrote about in Chapter 4: "Makiwara" of my book *Shotokan Myths*. You spend hours punching this darn thing. Bang! Bang! Bang! You put in more hip rotation, and the banging sound gets louder. Wow, this is wonderful! You love it! OK, I sound a little sarcastic, but this is the image of a tough *karateka* for many readers.

The eternal question is how to generate power in our karate techniques. So, the Shotokan masters of the twentieth century invented the concept of *kime*, which refers to total tension or focused power. You are supposed to achieve great power by tensing up all the muscles of your body. I refer to this as a myth in Chapter 1: "Kime" of *Shotokan Myths*. I am sure you have tried this but have found yourself being stiff and rigid instead of generating great power.

So, you may say, "OK, what else can we do, then?" Let me mention that one person also asked the same question some sixty or seventy years ago and discovered a method. His name was Shigeru Egami (江上茂, 1912– 1981 [photo right]), one of Funakoshi's disciples and the founder of the Shotokai. He believed that relaxing the upper body was the key requirement. His idea was to shift or take very quick steps without using *kime*. Watch video clips of the Shotokai *kata* and see how the performers move.

Egami believed in bending the front knee extremely far forward as seen in the picture to the left. In this stance, the center of gravity is much farther forward than in the standard stance we learn in JKA-style Shotokan. I suspect that, after trying many different ideas, Egami must have reached this conclusion based on the concept of *tokiho*, which I described earlier. By bending the front knee so far forward, you get to a point where you fall forward.

This makes sense, but the Shotokai never became a major Shotokan organization mainly because it denounced all tournaments. The JKA, on the other hand, became the dominant organization in the sixties and seventies but did not take up the concept of extreme knee bending, adopting instead the concept of *kime*. It is very interesting that these two organizations branched out from the same founder, Funakoshi, yet their respective concepts are so vastly different.

So, you will ask if I am proposing that we adopt this concept of extreme knee bending. My answer is yes and no. In *kihon kumite* such as *ippon kumite*, I think it is a good idea to adopt it as it will allow you to shift faster. It is also good to adopt low stances in *kata* to train your legs. So, I say yes to these exercises, particularly for junior students.

On the other hand, I say no to them for senior students. Adopting this stance in free sparring or in street-fighting situations is a joke. I have never seen how Shotokai practitioners fight in *jiyu kumite*, and they denounced tournaments. I suppose they believe in generating power by shifting quickly, not by extreme contraction of the upper body, but I would like to hear from Shotokai practitioners on this point for the sake of my own education.

In the end, what is my point? I simply want to point out the relationship between gravity and power. In the Shotokai, they have adopted extreme knee bending and relaxation of the upper body. In JKA-style Shotokan, we have adopted *kime*, which has made us look stiff and, in fact, move more slowly.

You may say, "Get to the point," and I will. We need to learn to move quickly as this generates power. Look at the picture to the left. I believe this is a picture of Takayuki Mikami (三上孝之, 1933– [on the right]) in one of the JKA's All Japan Championships of the late fifties. This is a perfect picture for showing how to generate power. You can see that his right fist is moving forward for an *oi zuki*. His opponent is standing straight up, so Mikami probably could have knocked this guy out if he wanted to. He did not need to put any power into his arm as his body movement was already carrying so much energy that this would have been a knock-out punch even without the additional force.

In a tournament, you must show a strong punch with your arm in order to score a point, but, in reality, a person who adopts this body position can simply extend his arm with little power in the arm itself and still produce a similar impact on the opponent. Of course, if you want to maximize the total power, adding the energy generated by the arm will help.

OK, so you understand that the benefits of gravity can give you speed and power. Some people may ask, "Why do I feel heavy, and why are my moves slow?" First of all, I must ask you, "Is your weight in line?" If you are overweight, then of course you feel heavy. Get light and stay slim. If your weight is in line, but you still feel slow, read Chapter 9: "Unstable Balance." To move fast in karate, the key is the initial movement, and this requires technique. Learn the concept and the technique, and then you will be able to make your initial move faster.

Then, how do you speed up the techniques? It all comes from relaxation. If you have unnecessary tension in your body, this will slow you down like the brakes on your car. Relaxation of the muscles is required to produce smooth and natural body movements, whether the movements are circular or linear.

I would like to add an observation about how *kumite* is being fought recently, particularly the *jiyu kumite* seen at tournaments, where I see two fighters continuously hopping all throughout the *kumite* match. When I was competing in the seventies, I rarely saw this style of fighting. However, I remember discussing this

topic with my karate friends in the seventies after we had seen one of Bruce Lee's movies, *The Way of the Dragon* (猛龍過江 [Golden Harvest, 1972]). This was released in the U.S. as *Return of the Dragon*, and Lee's opponent was Chuck

Norris, starring in his first big hit.

This mixed style of fighting took place in a dramatic scene at the Colosseum in Rome (photo on previous page). Some readers have probably seen this movie, but the story goes like this. Norris's character, Colt, is a good karate fighter and an assassin who is sent to kill Lee's character, Tang Lung. In the early part of the fight, Lee fights from a static stance, and Norris gets the better of him. So, after being beaten up, Lee changes his fighting style to a hopping style and, of course, wins in the end.

I thought it was interesting that Lee wrote the story in such a way that he wins by changing his fighting style, particularly to this hopping style. We laughed as we watched the movie because we thought his fighting style was funny as the change was drastic and unnatural. Even though I laughed at this scene, I thought Lee was an excellent movie director as he must have gotten this idea from the fighting style of Muhammad Ali (1942–2016), who was very popular in those years as he had light footing despite the fact that he was a heavyweight champion. Lee used this idea in his own movie even though this was not something he had learned from his Wing Chun master, Ip Man, in Hong Kong (photo left).

There seems to be a popular debate over whether or not Lee was a great martial artist. I will not go into this in this chapter, but I want to add my personal observation and evaluation. He definitely was a good actor, but I do not consider him to be a great martial artist as many people wish to believe. This is a controversial subject, and I am aware that my opinion does not make me popular or liked. I may touch on this subject in more detail sometime in the future and explain why I judge his skill level in the martial arts to be less than superior.

Let us go back to the current hopping style of *kumite*. As I mentioned earlier, the fighting style at tournaments in the seventies was different, and it changed somewhere in the mid eighties. Did it change because of this Bruce Lee movie?

No, I do not think that was the reason. Is this because it is a better fighting style? This is a tricky question, and my answer is yes and no.

I say yes because it works at most of the *kumite shiai* that we have these days, especially in WKF-style sport karate. Why is this so? One good reason is that hopping is used to hide attacking movements. It is used as a fake movement. In other words, if you are moving all the time, then it is difficult for the opponent to determine when an attack is going to be initiated. Another reason is that hopping requires some relaxation of the legs, which helps to generate fast leg movements.

It is true that after a hop, the bounced-off energy can be used to initiate a fast move forward. The hopping is also used like the idling of a car. Idling should be done within the body, but this requires a high level of skill, so most people have to use hopping for this action.

These are good points about the hopping action, but the main reason it is popular now is a change in the rules. The scoring standard was changed drastically when sport karate was introduced into the JKA in 1981, when it joined the World Union of Karate Organizations (世界空手連合 [WUKO]). I competed in the first WUKO national championship tournament in 1982, so I experienced this as I fought against practitioners of other styles, such as Shito Ryu and Goju Ryu. You can score with a much lighter punch now, but this kind of punch or kick would have been rejected for not having enough power in the *shiai* of the seventies. To score a point, we had to crouch low and jump forward with a punch or kick.

Which style is better is not the issue. One style is sport; the other is closer to *budo*. Look at wild animals. When a lion or a tiger hunts for prey, what does it do? It crouches and jumps forward when it attacks. You never see a lion or a tiger hopping around in an effort to catch

a deer. You will see hopping when dogs are play-
ing around but never when they fight. Just think
about if you were in a street fight, and your opponent had a knife or a stick. Would you still hop
as you fight?

Then, what is wrong with the hopping ac-
tion? First of all, from a martial arts perspective, the idea is not to show any intention of attacking, but this hopping action definitely shows one's intention to fight.
Secondly, when you hop into the air—unless this is being used to execute an attack—you are suspended, which is definitely a *suki* (隙), an opening or a moment
when it is most difficult to defend. Thirdly, if you hop in the same rhythm, your
opponent will learn your rhythm, which means a disadvantage to you. Enough said
about the *kumite* at the tournaments of recent years.

Conclusion

If you wish to move faster and generate extra power in your techniques, remember to do the following.

First of all, stay in shape and keep your body weight in line. Learn to relax
more, and train yourself to feel the center of gravity in your body, which we call
seichushin (正中心).

You must also train yourself to gain the ability to feel when you intentionally
break balance to move (in any direction). The more challenging part is knowing
the very point at which you tip from being balanced to being off-balance. The most
challenging part is staying at that strange and difficult point of being balanced in
a state of instability. By doing this, you are able to always be in a position or state
to move quickly.

To gain power, execute your techniques as you are moving toward the opponent or the target. Avoid executing techniques from a static stance or after your
body shifting has stopped as this is not the most effective use of gravity.

Now do you feel that gravity can be your friend and not so much your enemy? When you understand this, you will also understand why the ancient masters did not need to take low stances or any stance at all. They would assume a natural stance and then simply walk normally toward the opponent. That is the ultimate method for fast and strong techniques as it is in harmony with gravity.

押忍

CHAPTER ELEVEN
第十一章

THE MYSTERY OF THE KARATE MASTER
空手の達人の謎

What would one expect of a karate master upon meeting him? We know that Shotokan's *Dojo Kun* starts with perfection of character. If a practitioner is an eighth or ninth *dan* and has practiced karate for over forty years, which would mean he must have recited the *Dojo Kun* daily for all those years, wouldn't he be expected to be a person of high morals who is leading a healthy life?

A great example of a karate master is Gichin Funakoshi, the founder of Shotokan karate and typically called *The Father of Modern-Day Karate*. Funakoshi was in his fifties when he moved from Okinawa to Tokyo to introduce the Japanese people to karate. He was a retired teacher and could have enjoyed an easy retired life on Okinawa, but he chose to leave his entire family behind and lead a meager life in Tokyo until his death at eighty-nine years of age.

He did not have any friends nearby, let alone relatives, until his sons joined him many years later. As he mainly taught university students, he did not make much money. He certainly was not seeking fame or financial gain since karate was practically unknown in Japan when he introduced it in 1921. He was a dedicated person who desired only the recognition of this martial art and believed in the benefit of karate practice for the Japanese people. He never had a *dan* rank in his life and did not need a high rank to show he was a karate master. All the people who were associated with him came to respect him and consider him a true master.

Another good example is Masatoshi Nakayama, the founder and the first chief instructor of the JKA. He was widely respected not only by JKA members but also by practitioners of other styles and by other organizations.

When Japan lost World War II in 1945, the Allied forces banned all martial arts, including kendo, judo, and jujutsu. Kendo had to wait until the end of the occupation in 1952 to form the All Japan Kendo Federation (全日本剣

道連盟 [AJKF]), but Funakoshi and Nakayama worked together and were granted an exception to the rule, which allowed them to found the JKA in 1949. Nakayama was a man of character and a gentleman who respected all karate practitioners, whether Japanese or non-Japanese.

I am sure that all who read this will agree with what has been said about these two great masters, Gichin Funakoshi and Masatoshi Nakayama. In addition, I am sure there are other masters who are excellent in both karate and character. I personally know two sensei who were true masters. One was my first sensei, Jun Sugano (菅野淳, 1928–2002), ninth *dan* and former vice chairman of the JKA. The other was my last sensei, Tetsuhiko Asai (浅井哲彦, 1935–2006), tenth *dan* and founder of the Japan Karate Shoto Federation (日本空手松濤連盟 [JKS]).

Lack of space prevents me from explaining in detail why I consider these two to be true masters, but I can say a few things that I believe would be the qualifications of a true master. Both sensei were excellent at karate. I do not need to explain anything about Asai Sensei as he was globally known as a karate genius.

Sugano Sensei was not well known as he stayed away from the JKA headquarters and was not highly publicized. When he taught, none of his students wished to be picked when he would demonstrate a technique. His fist was like a hammer. He never hit hard, but you could feel it. He told me that Teruyuki Okazaki (岡崎照幸, 1931–), tenth *dan* and chairman of the International Shotokan Karate Federation (国際松濤館空手連盟 [ISKF]), was an excellent fighter but that Okazaki always avoided him during *kumite* training. This was during the 1960s, before Okazaki moved to the U.S.A.

Both sensei were firm and tough but never violent or abusive in their teaching. Their training was always challenging, unique, stimulating, and educational. Both of them were first-class educators and instructors. In addition, they were exemplary in their handling of money and power. The student's time and interest in karate were more important to them than his money. They were also disinterested in the titles and power that could be attained within the organizations to which they belonged. Sugano became a vice chairman of the JKA not because it was what he desired but because the board of directors unanimously recommended him based on his character.

Both Sugano and Asai were nonpolitical and accepted any practitioner from any organization or style. They were confident in their karate and were not motivated by financial gain.

So, were they perfect and without shortcomings? Unfortunately, that was not the case. Both of them had drinking problems when they were young, but, as far as anyone knows, there were never any embarrassing incidents due to their drinking habits. However, the heavy drinking of their youth certainly did cause them to be in an unhealthy condition when they reached their sixties and, unfortunately, shortened their lives. Both of them passed in their early seventies, which was too soon for them to go indeed.

Now, here is the big question: are these masters the standard for Shotokan karate? Unfortunately, this is not the case. Very sadly, I have heard more negative comments than positive ones about many karate "masters" during my trips around the world. Here is one of the frequent reports I have received: "Our dojo received some well-known instructors from Japan, and I expected them to behave like masters. Honestly, I was very disappointed in them. In fact, I was embarrassed sometimes by their behavior and actions."

This embarrassing behavior included a situation in which a "master" got heavily drunk, could not walk straight, and threw up in the restroom. I have even heard about another "master" who wanted to spend the night with a teenage female student. I also hear frequently about a certain "master" who behaves extremely aggressively to gain financial returns.

I have met many innocent (or maybe naïve) students who were shocked to see some of these "masters" chain smoking. These disappointed people tell me, "Why do they do this? I expected them to lead a healthy life and keep high moral standards." I can truly understand their confusion and disappointment. Such "masters" are all high-ranking sensei. Some reside in Japan, and others have emigrated and now live overseas.

I have witnessed some incidents myself and have heard many embarrassing and horrific stories. One story I can share comes from a Canadian instructor who invited a high-ranking Japanese instructor to visit from the U.S. The Japanese instructor demanded to be taken to the most expensive French restaurant in town, one where the average meal would cost several hundred dollars per person, especially since he planned to order a very expensive wine. The Japanese instructor liked the restaurant and demanded that the Canadian host take him there the following night. The host had to refuse his request as he was already in the red. The Japanese instructor did not show any understanding of the host's budgetary situation; he simply got very upset when his demand was not met.

Another story comes from Europe. One Japanese instructor suggested that a female student visit him before a *dan* exam if she wanted to pass. This visit was to take place in his hotel room the night before the exam. This story was hard for me to believe, but the person who told it to me said it was true.

As a Japanese karate instructor myself, I find this painfully embarrassing and feel that it is my responsibility to do something about it. Therefore, I feel that it is my duty to raise this subject and to solve the mystery of the master. I wish to share my knowledge with Western readers so that they will have the right expectations when it comes to karate masters. I hope I can shed some light on this mystery of Shotokan karate. (I specifically mention Shotokan karate as I have no knowledge or information on this subject as it pertains to other styles.)

Many people have been disappointed by what they have discovered in some of the masters. On the other hand, some people claim that the master's character is of little concern and that it is good enough if the practitioner is an expert in karate. According to these people, they are simply looking for karate skills, not a spiritual or moral leader, since this is not a religion. Even if the sensei's personality and behavior are poor, such people still respect him as a karate expert. They would ask, "Why do we expect karate masters to have high moral standards when we do not expect the same from coaches and trainers of other athletic events, such as boxing, wrestling, football, etc.?" For them, karate is simply a sport and nothing more.

I understand their point of view; however, many believe that karate can be more than a sport and can have additional benefits. For such people, what they practice is *karatedo* (空手道). The word *do* (道, 'way' or 'path') brings a different meaning to karate. It turns the whole learning and training process into a way of life. In *karatedo*, our goal of improvement does not stop with fighting skills but goes far beyond that to include our character, principles, and even outlook on life.

Karate skill is like a gun in that it is neutral in and of itself. It can be good or bad, depending on how it is used and by whom. If a policeman uses it to protect a citizen, then that gun is good. If a robber uses it in a bank robbery, then that gun is bad. Karate skill can be viewed in the same way. It can be good or bad, depending on how the practitioner uses it.

We may not expect our police officers to have perfection of character, but we definitely expect them to be honest and fair and to uphold justice. Would you accept a police officer who lies or is an alcoholic or a drug addict?

We also expect our police officers to be in shape, but that is another subject. Sadly, the national tendency toward obesity in the U.S. is also reflected in the police force. I have a great respect for the job of police officers and how they work to keep our society safe. However, when I see an overweight policeman, I ask myself, "Can he protect himself, let alone a civilian, if there is a fight or an encounter with criminals?" I chuckle to myself when I see that the prisoners in jail are overall in much better physical shape than many of the guards.

We must have high expectations for those masters teaching *karatedo*. Unfortu-

nately, many masters do not qualify. Why has thirty or forty years of karate training not automatically produced a practitioner with a high degree of character? It
is obvious that reciting the *Dojo Kun* thousands of times is not good enough. Let
me list several reasons that years of karate training have failed to create masters.

Reason 1

Karate, particularly Shotokan karate, became popular in the 1960s mainly because many young and powerful instructors were sent out by the JKA and the
Shotokai, many of whom later decided to immigrate to Western countries. Let's
look at the ages of some of these now-famous Shotokan experts who immigrated
to Europe and the U.S.A.

- Hidetaka Nishiyama (西山英峻, 1928–2008): moved to the U.S. in 1960
  at the age of thirty-two
- Teruyuki Okazaki (岡崎照幸, 1931–): moved to the U.S. in 1961 at the
  age of thirty
- Keinosuke Enoeda (榎枝慶之輔, 1935–2003): moved to the UK in 1965
  at the age of thirty
- Taiji Kase (加瀬泰治, 1929–2004): left Japan at the age of 35 to teach
  in countries such as South Africa, Germany, and Italy between 1964 and
  1966 before finally settling in France at the age of thirty-eight
- Hideo Ochi (越智秀男, 1940–): moved to Germa-
  ny in 1970 at the age of thirty
- Hiroshi Shirai (白井寛, 1937–): left Japan in 1965
  at the age of twenty-seven and made a world trip
  with Kase and Enoeda to promote karate before
  eventually settling in Milan, Italy
- Tsutomu Ohshima (大島劫, 1930– [photo right]):
  started karate training in 1948 and moved to Cali-

fornia, U.S.A., in 1955 at the age of twenty-five

- Mitsusuke Harada (原田満祐, 1928–): initially moved to Brazil in 1955 and then moved to the UK in 1963 at the age of thirty-five

In the 1950s and 1960s, Japan was extremely poor, and there were not enough jobs, especially for karate instructors. At that time, thousands immigrated to Brazil, Bolivia, Hawaii, Peru, etc., to become farmers. It was a very natural course of action for a hungry population to think of emigration.

Those who emigrated had to be very young since older people would not be able to endure the anticipated poor and harsh living conditions. The same thing was true of karate instructors. They were very young when they left Japan without any support from the organizations to which they belonged. They were totally on their own as far as their financial situation was concerned. Harada was probably the only exception as he got a position with the Bank of South America in São Paulo, Brazil, in 1955.

In the 1960s, the JKA was so poor that it could not even pay its instructors in Tokyo a sufficient salary, so it was impossible for it to send any money to its overseas instructors. I believe this situation had a great impact on how these instructors developed their minds and how they conducted the business aspect of karate operations.

I am not questioning whether or not any of the instructors listed above would qualify as masters. Other than Okazaki, I have not known any of these instructors personally, so I cannot judge if they are or are not true masters. I only know them by what is publicly known to all of us. If any of these instructors failed to achieve the true qualities of a master, then their living conditions must have been a part of the cause.

Reason 2

Many instructors consider karate a full-time job. This, in and of itself, is not necessarily bad or wrong as it is certainly fair for them to ask for monetary compensation for their teaching. I have been teaching karate since the early 1970s, but I have always had a separate full-time job and kept karate as a part-time job so that I would not fall into the trap of being tempted by money.

When an instructor begins to look at his students as customers and the means by which he attains a comfortable life, his whole attitude and behavior will change. He will have to compromise and make many concessions. His main interest will become making money from the students. The amount of attention given to the development of the students' karate level will become very questionable. I have heard of a few masters who are known for selling *dan* ranks. If an instructor is paying more attention to your money than to your karate skills, then that instructor must not be called *master*.

Reason 3

Why would a high-ranking instructor from a globally recognized organization do embarrassing things? I know this is puzzling to many readers, but I think part of the blame falls on Western people. This may come as a surprise to some readers, but I am not passing the buck to Westerners entirely, either.

Remember how you adored those Japanese masters and put them on a pedestal some thirty or forty years ago? Without exaggeration, some instructors were treated like gods. They quickly got used to this, which resulted in arrogance and unrealistic expectations. Once they started to act like gods, it became more difficult for Westerners to say no and to change.

Some Westerners have confessed to me, "We assumed that kind of thing was normal in Japan, so we believed we had to do it." I have told them that even if that were the case in Japan (though it isn't), they should not permit it if such behavior is not acceptable or reasonable in their own countries. Japanese instructors must respect the cultures and etiquette of the countries they are visiting or in which they are residing.

Even though I am a Japanese instructor myself, I call what is not right, wrong. Thus, I recommend that Western people who host Japanese instructors stand up and refuse any unreasonable requests that the latter may make. Japanese instructors need to come down to a human level and be treated equally.

Will this be considered disrespectful? No, not if you communicate it respectfully. Of course, you cannot treat them like hired consultants, either. Instructors have a good deal of self-pride, and the services they offer are not a commercial product. However, it is still a business proposition, so it is wise to clarify what has been agreed upon and what is unacceptable. Though, ideally, these matters would be discussed and clarified prior to the instructor's visit, in many cases, the requests and demands come after the instructor has arrived. If a request from an instructor exceeds what you have agreed to, or if it is unacceptable, it is best to express this honestly and clearly.

Master Funakoshi was a gentleman. He wanted to teach karate to university students as a way for them to develop courage and etiquette. He knew these were qualities that were necessary to the formation of a gentleman. However, to his disappointment, he must have found that some students did not follow his example.

First of all, university students had only four years to learn karate, which was far too little time to learn the true essence of karate, even if they practiced every day for the whole four years. Some of them would drop out after only a couple of years of karate training, not enough time for them to become proficient but long enough for them to become bullies.

In the pre–World War II era, military factions ruled the Japanese government, and university students were candidates for future military service as officers, so tough or macho behavior was encouraged in these students. Master Funakoshi did not want to teach karate for students to end up turning into thugs or violent officers. He could not preach much as he would sound as if he were going against what the military department wanted, so his solution was to introduce the *Dojo Kun*, which contained the five principles he believed in, and he made it a rule that all students would recite these five principles after every training session.

These *kun* are short, but they are the essence of Funako-shi karate. This tradition has been handed down for decades. Master Funakoshi himself set the example of how a gentle-man should live. He might have created many gentleman *karateka* before World War II, but many of them were killed during a war in which Japan was devastated.

When the war ended, and when Japanese organizations started to dispatch their instructors, Japan was an extremely poor third-world country. This seems almost unbelievable to us when we consider the prosperity Japan enjoys today.

The Japanese instructors who were dispatched overseas, to be frank, were neither well prepared nor well educated. They were poor, and few of them were educated to be gentlemen. They were, in fact, very young, in their twenties and thirties, with no more than just ten to fifteen years of karate training behind them. I do not mean to single out Ohshima, but, in his case, he had merely seven years of karate training (1948–1955).

These young instructors were sent out into a world where people knew very little about karate. They were fast and strong; many of the ones from the JKA were national champions in Japan. They had become masters in a short period of time.

I do not know if these masters continued their training in order to improve their character and deserve the title of *master*. I feel that they were obligated to demonstrate the principles of the *Dojo Kun* and to lead their students by example, as Master Funakoshi did. Unfortunately, some became arrogant and power hungry.

Some chose to be politicians and businessmen in order to expand their territories and their financial gains.

Many Western practitioners now have more than thirty or even forty years of hard karate training under their belt. I dare say that their level is equivalent, if not superior, to that of the original Japanese instructors when they immigrated to the U.S. and Europe. The responsibility of Western instructors is to not repeat the mistakes that some Japanese instructors have made during the last forty years. I sincerely hope that Western instructors will strive to reach higher not only in the quest for karate skill but also in the principles of the *Dojo Kun*.

What do Western instructors need to do to reach the ultimate goal? Here are some requirements:

1. Improve real karate skills. If you are thirty or forty years old and have just retired from the tournament circuit, do not stop training. Now is the time to start practicing real karate and training more. Frankly speaking, tournament karate is only a small part of karate. There is much more than just *gyaku zuki* and *mae geri*. Learn and acquire higher skills, such as *ikken hissatsu* (一拳必殺, 'one punch, certain kill'), *sunkei* (寸勁, one-inch punch), *tenketsu* (点穴, '*dim mak*'), and ki (気).

一拳必殺

2. Continue to train daily and maintain a high level of karate skill until you are in your seventies, eighties, and beyond. Do not injure your knees and back from incorrect training. Real masters must be able to demonstrate excellent technique when they are in their seventies, just as Master Asai did. If you are in your fifties or sixties, then you must not make excuses

by saying, "I used to be able to do this or that." Karate is always what you can do now and never how it was before.

3. Learn to separate karate from money. Do not make karate into a business so that you can teach what you believe in with no fear of losing students. It is best to have a separate business or a full-time job so that your living is not dependent on the income from karate. When an instructor sells a *dan* rank, he sells his soul. Do not sell your soul if you wish to be a true master.

4. Stay away from the politics of karate. It will take too much valuable time away from your own training and teaching. People follow you because your karate is truly excellent, not because you are a big shot in a large organization.

5. Study kinesiology and physiology so that you understand how the body works. Through thorough knowledge and understanding of the body and its mechanisms, we can not only move our body in the most effective way but also teach and share this knowledge properly.

6. Study the history of karate and expand your experience to other martial arts. You will have a much better understanding of your karate by learning how Shotokan was created and how other martial arts are related. Learn how other styles of karate are practiced and compare them to your practice of Shotokan karate. By doing this, you will have a much better understanding of Shotokan karate, and you will be able to expand this to something beyond, as Master Asai did.

Some readers may ask, "Can a Western instructor really become a karate master?" My answer is very clear: "Yes, it is very possible." A karate master does not need to be Japanese or Asian. If a Western instructor can develop all the qualities and abilities necessary, then he certainly can be a karate master.

It would please me greatly to see many true karate masters among the Western *karateka* in the future. Furthermore, I would love to see some of those Western karate masters teach Japanese students and show them true *budo* karate. Should that happen, I am sure many narrow-minded Japanese instructors would be upset, but I sincerely hope that such a surprising turn of events would be a wake-up call for them. It would be very beneficial to Japanese karate if it could make them realize that they cannot be arrogant and lazy. That would benefit not only Japanese karate but also the karate of the entire world.

押忍

CHAPTER TWELVE
第十二章

SHUHARI
守破離

Shuhari is not a concept that enjoys as much popularity as *karatedo*, *budo*, or Zen (禅) in the Western world. In Japan, on the other hand, this is a fairly popular concept not only in the martial arts but in all arts. *Wikipedia* describes it as follows (as of September 2016):

> *Shuhari* (Kanji: 守破離 Hiragana: しゅはり) is a Japanese martial art concept, and describes the stages of learning to mastery. It is sometimes applied to other Japanese disciplines, such as Go.

It further describes the meaning of the concept, using the following statement by aikido master Seishiro Endo (遠藤征四郎, 1942–):

> It is known that, when we learn or train in something, we pass through the stages of *shu*, *ha*, and *ri*. These stages are explained as follows. In *shu*, we repeat the forms and discipline ourselves so that our bodies absorb the forms that our forbears created. We remain faithful to these forms with no deviation. Next, in the stage of *ha*, once we have disciplined ourselves to acquire the forms and movements, we make innovations. In this process the forms may be broken and discarded. Finally, in *ri*, we completely depart from the forms, open the door to creative technique, and arrive in a place where we act in accordance with what our heart/mind desires, unhindered while not overstepping laws.

The explanation above is not sufficient, so I will attempt to put more meat on its bones. Before I go into the deeper meaning of the concept of *shuhari*, I would like to share some background information about how it began.

The person who started this concept was Fuhaku Kawakami (川上不白, 1719–1807), who was born into a samurai family and was raised as a samurai until the age of sixteen. There is nothing unusual about his early life, but what happened later in his life made him unique and interesting.

When he was sixteen, his samurai master ordered him to become a student of Joshinsai (如心斎, 1705–1751), a famous tea master in Kyoto who was the seventh generation of the Omotesenke (表千家). The master's order was for him not only to learn the art of the tea ceremony but to become a teacher of the tea ceremony, which he did when he was thirty-one years old. This age sounds young to us, but you need to remember that the average life expectancy at that time was under fifty years, so thirty-one was definitely not considered young then.

To earn the title of *tea master*, Kawakami had to spend fifteen years of his life totally dedicated to the pursuit of the mastery of the tea ceremony. After receiving his teaching credential, he started teaching the tea ceremony in Edo (modern-day Tokyo), and his style is called *Edo Senke* (江戸千家).

I suspect that Western readers probably wonder why in the world a samurai master would order his man to do something that seems to have nothing to do with the samurai or the martial arts. Maybe some readers are into Japanese history and the culture of the samurai. Some may already know the relationship between the samurai and the tea ceremony. For many others, why the tea ceremony became so important to the samurai may be a mystery.

To understand this, we need to take a look at the unique features of the *chashitsu* (茶室, 'tearoom'). Before the *Sengoku* (戦国, 'Warring States') period, the space of a tearoom was somewhat larger, measuring four and a half *jo* (畳). The character 畳 refers to the tatami, a straw mat the Japanese use as a floor covering, and, when read as *jo*, it is also used to measure the size of a room. For instance, if you say, "My room is six *jo*," this means that six tatami will fit in your room. One tatami is roughly 35 inches by 70 inches (88 centimeters by 176 centimeters). For the convenience of putting these mats in a room, the width is exactly half the length. The typical room is a six-mat room, and a four-and-a-half-mat room is considered small.

Anyway, as the Sengoku period started, the activity known as *chanoyu* (茶の湯, 'the tea ceremony'), became very popular among the samurai and was devel-

oped into *sado* (茶道, 'the way of tea'). Interestingly, as *sado* became more popular, the room size shrank. The typical *chashitsu* is now three mats. It can barely
accommodate the ceremony master, one or two guests, and a small hearth for the
boiling water. The concept here is simplicity and frugality. This also allows the
ceremony master and his guests to enjoy the closeness between them.

The heritage of this concept is still visible in Japan today. If you have visited
Japan in recent years, you will have noticed this. You do not even need to visit
somebody's house. You will find hotel rooms to be comparatively smaller than
those found in the U.S. and Europe. If you visit restaurants in Tokyo, you will really feel the closeness of the other customers. You sit so close to the next customer
that sometimes you cannot even raise your elbow to eat.

More interestingly, the entrance to
the *chashitsu* is less than a square yard
(square meter) in size (photo left), which
is so small that the master and guests
must crawl into the room. The idea is
that this entrance forces every partici-
pant to bow down and teaches everyone
to be humble.

This tradition has also been carried over to modern times. In front of many restaurants in Japan, you will find a cloth that looks like a flag being flown sideways at
the entrance. This cloth is not to keep the flies from entering the shop as you rarely
see flies in Japan. It is typically used to advertise the store's name, which is dyed
into it. These days, a restaurant can have a bigger sign on the roof, so they do not
really need this cloth, but they maintain this tradition while foreigners wonder why
they have this annoying thing in front of the restaurant. It is interesting as everyone
has to bow to go into the restaurant, even if he is a customer.

OK, now you understand that simplicity and humility are an integral part of
chanoyu, and you can see how these character traits would impress the samurai.
But, it is still not clear why the samurai took the tea ceremony so seriously. Believe

it or not, it is because of one aspect of the tea ceremony: *ichigo ichie* (一期一会).
Indeed, this concept touched the hearts of the samurai. Let us find out what it is all
about. Here I will quote the explanation of this cultural concept from *Wikipedia* (as
of September 2016), which can be read at www.wikipedia.org/wiki/Ichi-go_ichi-e:

Ichigo ichie (一期一会 "one time, one meeting")
is a Japanese four-character idiom (*yojijukugo*) that
describes a cultural concept of treasuring meetings
with people. The term is often translated as "for
this time only," "never again," or "one chance in a
lifetime." The term reminds people to cherish any
gathering that they may take part in, citing the fact
that many meetings in life are not repeated. Even
when the same group of people can get together again, a particular gathering will
never be replicated and thus, each moment is always once-in-a-lifetime. The concept
is most commonly associated with Japanese tea ceremonies, especially tea masters
Sen no Rikyū and Ii Naosuke.

It goes on to say the following:

Ichigo ichie is linked with Zen Buddhism and concepts of transience. The term is particularly associated with the Japanese tea ceremony, and is often brushed onto scrolls
which are hung in the tea room.

  The term is also much repeated in *budō* (martial ways). It is sometimes used to
admonish students who become careless or frequently stop techniques midway to "try
again," rather than moving on with the technique despite the mistake. In a life-or-death
struggle, there is no chance to "try again." Even though techniques may be attempted
many times in the dojo, each should be seen as a singular and decisive event. Similarly,
in *noh* theater, performances are only rehearsed together once, a few days before the
show, rather than the many times that are typical in the West, this corresponding to the
transience of a given show.

I am afraid the explanation above is not sufficient to explain the relationship
between the samurai and the tea ceremony. This concept is critical in understand-

ing the relationship between these two, and it must be explained further, so I will add my own explanation as to how this concept really came to be in tune with the mind of the samurai in the seventeenth and eighteenth centuries.

In the seventeenth century, Japan was going through the previously mentioned Warring States period, a time of social upheaval, political intrigue, and nearly constant military conflict that lasted roughly from the middle of the fifteenth century to the beginning of the seventeenth century. During this period of nearly two hundred years, the main island of Japan was filled with wars. Tens of thousands of samurai had to go into battle almost every year. Certainly, many were killed, and there was no guarantee regarding their fate or their survival when the wars were coming so successively.

There was a general feeling of transience, and they felt that their life was very fleeting. But, instead of becoming despondent and giving up, they tried to overcome this and attempted to attain calmness of mind by realizing the fact that they were living at that very moment, *ichigo ichie*. It is interesting as this realization and way of thinking is something that bears some similarity to that found among the hippies of the sixties, when the U.S. was going through the Vietnam War. Instead of smoking marijuana, the samurai took to drinking tea and called it *chanoyu* ('the tea ceremony') or *sado* ('the way of tea').

Anyway, there are strict manners and a method of conduct in *chanoyu*. You are to follow the strict code of behavior of receiving the cup from the ceremony master with a steady hand and then slowly taking a sip. After drinking a small amount of tea, you return the cup to the ceremony master (again, with a steady hand). If your mind is not calm, this behavior cannot be done in a very smooth and steadily controlled motion.

The samurai liked Zen meditation, as

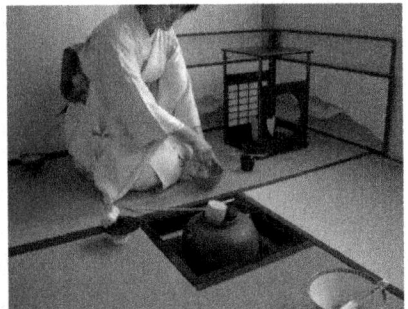

well, for gaining concentration and a feeling of detachment. But, they preferred *chanoyu* as going through the ceremony was easier and more fulfilling because they could interact with the ceremony master. Also, back then, the samurai did not know about the health benefits of tea that we now know of, but they must have instinctively felt the goodness of drinking tea.

The following is an article entitled "The Proof Is In: Drinking Tea Is Healthy" from the October 2004 edition of *Harvard Women's Health Watch*:

Although tea drinking has been associated with health benefits for centuries, only in recent years have its medicinal properties been investigated scientifically. The October issue of *Harvard Women's Health Watch* recognizes the healthy power of tea while helping readers get the most out of their cups.

Tea's health benefits are largely due to its high content of flavonoids—plant-derived compounds that are antioxidants. Green tea is the best food source of a group called *catechins*. In test tubes, catechins are more powerful than vitamins C and E in halting oxidative damage to cells and appear to have other disease-fighting properties. Studies have found an association between consuming green tea and a reduced risk for several cancers, including skin, breast, lung, colon, esophageal, and bladder.

Additional benefits for regular consumers of green and black teas include a reduced risk for heart disease. The antioxidants in green, black, and oolong teas can help block the oxidation of LDL (bad) cholesterol, increase HDL (good) cholesterol and improve artery function. A Chinese study published recently in the *Archives of Internal Medicine* showed a 46%–65% reduction in hypertension risk in regular consumers of oolong or green tea, compared to nonconsumers of tea.

The October issue provides a few tips to get the most out of tea drinking:

- Drink a cup of tea a few times a day to absorb antioxidants and other healthful plant compounds. In green-tea drinking cultures, the usual amount is three cups per day.
- Allow tea to steep for three to five minutes to bring out its catechins.
- The best way to get the catechins and other flavonoids in tea is to drink it freshly brewed. Decaffeinated, bottled ready-to-drink tea preparations, and instant teas have less of these compounds.
- Tea can impede the absorption of iron from fruits and vegetables. Adding lemon or milk or drinking tea between meals will counteract this problem.

In addition, according to hypnotherapist Sara Maude Brighton, there are definitely some physiological effects of caffeine. She writes the following in her newsletter:

The main ingredient in coffee that gives us that boost is caffeine, a central nervous system stimulant. Caffeine is found naturally in tea, chocolate, fizzy drinks, and even in pain killers and weight-control drugs.

Caffeine stimulates the central nervous system by blocking adenosine, a neurotransmitter that normally causes a calming effect in the body. The resulting neural stimulation due to this blockage causes the adrenal glands to release adrenaline, the "fight-or-flight" hormone. Your heart rate increases, your pupils dilate, your muscles tighten up, and glucose is released into your blood stream for extra energy.

So, the samurai found *chanoyu* to be very beneficial both physically and mentally. When they came across with the concept of *ichigo ichie*, it certainly struck the core of their psyche.

Now let us look further into the concept of our main subject, *shuhari*. I quote one Japanese explanation from the kenjutsu book *Katsujinken Battodo* (活人剣抜刀道 [Soubunsha, 1995]) by Taizaburo Nakamura (中村泰三郎). I will also offer my English translation under each section of Japanese text.

伝統を受け継ぐ者にとって忘れてはならない、特に武道にとっての教えが「守破離」である。

Shuhari is a teaching principle that must not be forgotten by the carrier of the heritage, especially in martial arts.

「守」とは、師や各流派の教えを忠実に守り、それからはずれることのないように精進して身につけよ、という意味である。

Shu represents the concept that, for many years, one must follow and adhere to the teachings of his instructor and his style without making any changes or modifications.

「破」とは、今まで学んで身につけた教えから一歩進めて他流の教え、技を取り入れることを心がけ、師から教えられたものにこだわらず、さらに心と技を発展させよ、という意味である。

Ha means that, after mastering the teachings from his teacher, he must expand what he has learned by exposing himself to other styles and teachers. Here he must introduce other techniques and concepts so that he can improve his physical and mental skills to reach the next level.

「離」とは、破からさらに修行して、守にとらわれず破も意識せず、新しい世界を拓き、独自のものを生みだせ、という意味である。

Ri is the final stage, which he reaches only after decades of ha practice. Here he no longer gets influenced by the teachings of his past teachers. He opens his own world and his style.

「守破離」は単に武道の世界だけの教えではない。学問も経営も技術も、すべてにあてはまる。師に教えられて師に止まっていては発展はない。古武道に出発して古武道の中で止まっていたのでは、後継者としての存在価値はない。師をしのぎ、伝統を越え、親を超越して、より高い次元に発展成長してこそ文明の進歩がある。「守破離」とはその意味の言葉である。

The concept of shuhari does not apply only to the martial arts. It can apply to any education, business, or craft. There is no progress if you stop at the teaching of your teacher. There is no value to the inheritor of kobudo if he stays only inside of kobudo. The advancement of culture comes only when a person exceeds his teacher and parents and develops the traditions to a higher realm. Shuhari is the concept of this teaching.

It is difficult to know the exact number of years or amount of training for each category, but my understanding is that at least ten to fifteen years should be spent for shu. For ha, it is more difficult as the value of the additional learning, as well as the level of talent possessed by each practitioner, will vary so much. I would say that one must spend at least thirty to forty years in the ha stage before he can explore the ri stage.

I may be conservative with these time requirements, but I feel that this much time is needed by the average practitioner, such as myself. I must be untalented because I have been practicing Shotokan karate for nearly fifty years, yet I do not feel that I am anywhere near the *ri* stage. I am already sixty-nine years old (as of 2016), and I do not know when I will ever be able to reach the *ri* stage. Of course, for a talented practitioner such as the late Master Asai, probably less than half that time would be required; however, I consider him to be an exception, so he should not be the standard.

For the average practitioner, it is very possible that he may never reach the *ri* stage. This is a very important point. *Shu* and *ha* are the stages that almost all practitioners can attain, but only the talented ones can reach the *ri* stage. Just spending fifty or sixty years in karate does not automatically qualify you to get to the *ri* stage. In order to do this, you must be better than not only your own sensei but also all the sensei in Shotokan. If you believe that you are as good as, or better than, Okazaki, Nishiyama, Enoeda, Kase, Nakayama, and Funakoshi, then I guess you can claim that you are at the *ri* stage. This is my definition, and I believe this is the way *shuhari* is understood in Japan.

I would like to point out two interesting facts that I have observed in the karate world in Japan and the U.S. As I am not as familiar with the karate world in Europe and other regions, I will limit my comments to the experiences I have had in Japan and the U.S., where I have been teaching for more than fifty years. The situation is very similar in all of the mainstream Shotokan organizations in Japan and the U.S., including the JKA, JSKA, SKIF, JKS, ISKF, and a few others.

The two facts that I mentioned above are that, according to my experience and observations, most Japanese practitioners' training menus keep them in the *shu* stage too long, and they either are unable or do not know how to move on to the *ha* stage. Most American practitioners, on the other hand, tend to move through the *shu* stage too quickly and sometimes even jump straight into the *ri* stage, skipping the *ha* stage entirely. This is seen in some practitioners who even create their own *kata* for tournaments, etc.

I came across an interesting saying posted by a Shotokan practitioner on my

Facebook wall. It goes like this: "A black belt is a white belt who did not give up." I sort of understand what this statement is trying to say and give it credit as an attractive saying. It is true that over ninety percent of white belts quit before they reach *shodan*. But, there are many reasons that almost all beginners eventually drop out, and all of the fault—if there is such a thing—should not fall on the practitioners alone. The responsibility must be carried by the instructors and the organizations. There are, unfortunately, many poor and unqualified instructors who demotivate or discourage new students, and most of the major organizations have restrictive policies and practice sectionalism.

After ten or fifteen years of karate training at the *shu* level, a practitioner probably becomes a *nidan* or *sandan*. At this stage, he should start exploring the *ha* level, where he will be exposed to not only other instructors but also other karate styles and other kinds of martial arts. But, the fact is that the members of these organizations are not only discouraged from trying this but are punished if they do so. Yes, they are punished for wanting to learn and expand their karate.

This was one of the main reasons I resigned from the JKA and the ISKF. Kanazawa Kancho, of the SKIF, is very active in tai chi, so I suspect there is some influence there, but, based on what I witnessed at the seminars he gave in the nineties and the few years immediately following, I have discovered very few differences between their syllabus and that of the JKA.

Some readers may be surprised that I included even the JKS in the list. This organization was started by Tetsuhiko Asai in 2000, and I joined in 2002 because it was different. The organization had a lot more to offer, such as Junro (順路) *kata* and Asai-style *kihon* and *kumite*. However, after the passing of Asai Sensei in 2006, the organization started to go backward. It began to de-emphasize Asai Sensei's additions, and its syllabus became similar to that of the JKA. That was the main reason I resigned from that organization in 2009.

When I introduce mainstream practitioners to Asai *kata*, I get two types of reactions. One group is positive and appreciates the different body movements that are required in Asai *kata*. The other group is negative and rejects the *kata*, saying, "The JKA's twenty-six *kata* are already too many, and I have no room for any more." I agree with this statement if it comes from a *shodan*, a *nidan*, or even a *sandan*. But, if you are a *yondan* or above, don't you think it is about time to take on the responsibility of getting into the *ha* stage? I seriously hope all senior instructors will be brave enough to expand their experience and perspective.

At the other extreme, I see some practitioners in their thirties and forties who start their own styles. This may not be a common occurrence, but what I often see in many American practitioners is a lack of patience for staying in the *shu* stage for the necessary minimum of ten to fifteen years.

There are several different reasons and causes. One is that American people are very creative. In other words, they want to do their own thing. This good character trait can backfire, though, if they do not stick with the basics and original teachings long enough. They will have either a weak foundation or no foundation on which to build anything credible or meaningful.

Secondly, for an American, ten or fifteen years is a very long time, and it is extremely difficult for him to stick to the same thing for that long. His country's history itself spans only two hundred years or so. Compare this to that of Japan, which easily exceeds twenty centuries.

Thirdly, American society is highly mobile. Again, I am limiting my analysis to U.S. society as I am not familiar with the socioeconomics of Europe. Most U.S. citizens continually move due to school- and work-related reasons. According to *Ask.com*, the average American moves every five years. In Japan, however, it is not rare to see a family living not only in the same city but in the very same house for many generations.

Fourthly, change is good in the U.S., which has much less respect for tradition.

So, for these reasons, American practitioners have difficulty staying at the same dojo, or even in the same style, even if it offers a high level of karate training. I have come across so many *soke* (宗家) in the U.S. karate world.

This is my overall impression, and it is definitely not conclusive or definitive in the case of all dojo and organizations. I am speaking of a general trend that I have witnessed as I have visited many different dojo and tournaments in Japan and the U.S. These were mostly Shotokan, but some were other styles.

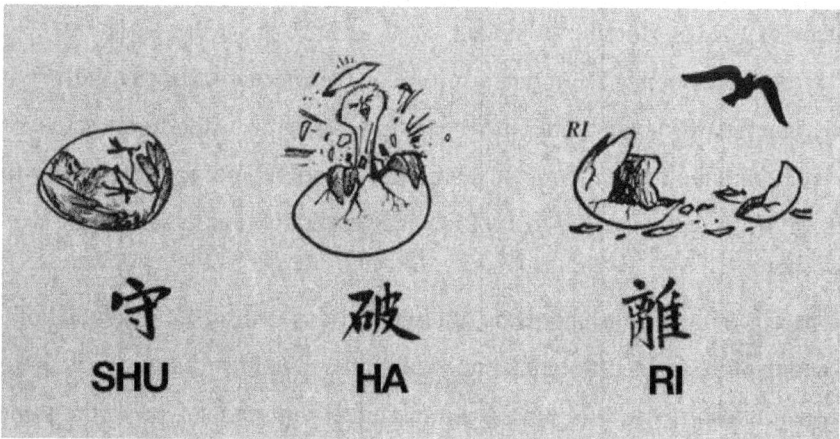

SHU   HA   RI

Conclusion

I see a serious problem with practitioners who cut corners and try to get into the *ha* stage prematurely. I can understand that trying new things is exciting and, in a way, educational. However, I still say to these people that their progress will stop in the middle of the *ha* stage as they have not perfected their foundation, that is, the *shu* stage, and they will never be able to reach the true *ri* stage. While you are below the *nidan* level, you need to be patient and focus all your time and energy on perfecting the *kihon* and *kata* of your school or style.

On the other hand, I see a bigger problem with practitioners in large mainstream organizations. Even if my advice to explore happens to reach them, their hands are sort of tied by the rules and policies of their organization.

I was one of them for almost forty years. In the first twenty years, I did not even see the problem. In the latter twenty years, I tried to forget about the problem and stay isolated, but this was not good. In the end, I almost gave up on karate. In fact, I totally stayed away from karate for four years, during which time I did not wear a *karategi* (空手着) even once.

The big change came when I participated in one of Asai Sensei's seminars. It took me a year before I could resign from the JKA and the ISKF, but I am glad that I did. I am nowhere near the *ri* stage, but I am truly enjoying my freedom and the excitement of exploring the *ha* stage.

If you have spent fifteen years in one of these organizations, and if you are totally happy with your karate, then there is no need to listen to me. However, if you feel you have reached your plateau after practicing the same thing for fifteen years, and you feel you need to explore and expand, I want to send these words to you: "Be brave."

There is a bigger world outside of organizations and styles. Take the bold next step and explore and learn. I guarantee that this will help and improve your karate. Even if it doesn't, you will have lost nothing. If you had stayed in the same rut, you would only remain there. This is my sincere hope, that more Shotokan practitioners will get their feet wet and see that it is not a criminal act to experience the *ha* stage.

押忍

CHAPTER THIRTEEN
第十三章

TENKETSU JUTSU
点穴術

Tetsuhiko Asai was a true genius in the martial arts, and his mastery of karate was far beyond what we know of Shotokan karate. His story has been told by many, and there are many video clips to show his amazing techniques in karate and other martial arts, including weapons. But, here I would like to share a story about a technique of his that has not been told much in Japan and has never been told in the Western world. This is about his mastery of *tenketsu jutsu*.

The reader should not be embarrassed if he has never heard this term before. In fact, this word cannot be found on *Wikipedia*, so you could safely say that the word is not known in the Western world. However, many readers will probably recognize the Chinese pronunciation, *dim mak*, as this latter term enjoys a long explanation on *Wikipedia*. Well known it may be, but, at the same time, its history in the U.S., starting in the sixties with a certain American character named *Count Dante* (1939–1975), is not so reputable. Another term that is used is *kyushojutsu*, which may sound more familiar to some readers.

I want to emphasize that I am a realist and do not believe in mystical concepts or other so-called mumbo jumbo. Before I dive into *tenketsu*, let me share an experience I had while on my search for extraordinary martial arts techniques.

In the nineties, I learned about Master Kozo Nishino (西野皓三, 1926–), who was an expert in the area of ki. He had such strong ki that he could use it to flip people around without touching them. I read all the books he had written and purchased a few videotapes. His performance in the videos truly amazed me as he could throw people left and right (not just a few, but ten or twenty people simultaneously). Some of the people would flip and jump as though they had been blasted by an explosive. In the video, he was easily able to knock a person down without touching him.

This technique is called *toate* (遠当て). *To* (遠) means 'far', and *ate* (当て) means 'hit', so this term literally means 'hitting [someone] from afar'. Here is a

YouTube video of a demonstration against some high school students: www.you-tube.com/watch?v=RLBa0ie1T-Q.

Interesting, isn't it? I am a believer in the existence of ki, but I did not believe one could have ki strong enough to knock down another individual. So, after viewing these demonstrations in the mid nineties, I believed in Master Nishino's ability and wished to learn the technique. I concluded that *toate* would be the ultimate karate punching technique.

I found a job in Japan in 1997 and moved back to Tokyo to live there for nearly three years. As soon as I moved to Tokyo, I joined Nishino Dojo in Shibuya. The training fee was extremely expensive, but I took two classes a week.

As I expected, Master Nishino could flip hundreds of students at will just like in the video mentioned above. It was amazing and very impressive to watch him in action. The reactions of the students were not fake, but genuine. They were regular citizens of all ages and occupations. They were paying hundreds of dollars each month to learn ki, so there was no reason they would pretend to be flipped around.

One very unfortunate thing was that there was only one student Master Nishino could not throw or move with his ki, and I was that student. The funny thing is that the other students looked at me as though something were wrong with me. I was totally disappointed as I really wanted to feel his ki and experience the ki flip without being touched. Though I tried very hard, I did not feel anything at all when he pointed his hands at me. He even touched me and pushed my arm in the ki-exchange form (i.e., with our forearms crossed and touching as in the kung fu pushing-hand exercise [photo right]). He got frustrated and told me I was too stiff and was resisting his ki. I did not argue with him, but my situation was the exact

opposite. I was totally relaxed and was more than willing to be flipped around.

Master Nishino would come to the dojo once a week. On that day, all the students would line up in front of him to receive his ki. After finding that he could not move me, he changed his days at the dojo. He came only on the days when I was not scheduled. I changed my dates so that I could be in his class. To make a long story short, in the end, Master Nishino asked me to stop coming to his class. He told me that I was too nervous and that my mind was too stiff. So, I quit the school and gave up learning the *toate* technique after two years of training at his dojo.

I can say that his technique was not universal; thus, I concluded that it was not something I wanted to learn. After this experience, I remained a nonbeliever in mystical powers and techniques, and I certainly had that attitude when I visited Asai Sensei soon after the close of the twentieth century.

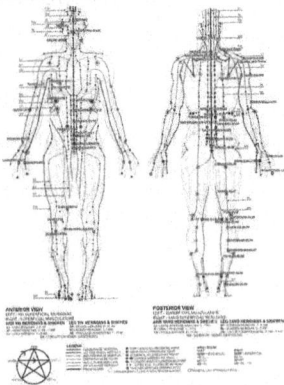

Human body meridians

Before I talk about my experience with Asai Sensei, let's look into the definition of *tenketsu* (*dim mak*) so that we will have a better understanding of what this technique is all about. *Dim mak* is written in Traditional Chinese as 點脈 and in Simplified Chinese as 点脉. The first character, 點/点, means 'spot', and the second, 脈/脉, means 'pulse', 'vein', or 'artery'. *Wikipedia* translates the compound term as 'press artery' or 'pressure point'.

This technique is also written as 点穴, which is read as *tenketsu* in Japanese. The first character, 点, is the simplified version of 點 with the same meaning, 'spot' or 'point'. The second character, 穴, means 'hole' or 'tunnel'. As you can guess, its history can be traced back to acupuncture.

Tenketsu is also called *kyushojutsu* (急所術, 'vital point techniques') in Japan. In the martial arts, it is explained that these techniques are used to attack pressure points or vital points.

According to *Wikipedia*, the word *dim mak* was introduced into America in the sixties and became well known in American pop culture in the eighties. However, most practitioners and masters were fakes, and this word became a joke, so many people believe this only exists in fairy tales or is simply mumbo jumbo. I want to share an actual experience that I had with the art that was performed by Asai Sensei and leave it up to the reader to decide if such techniques exist or not.

Tenketsu has never been widely published in the Western world. In fact, it is not very well known even in Japan. Luckily, a major Japanese magazine, *Karate-Do*, published an article on Asai Sensei and his *tenketsu* techniques in its February 2002 issue. A translation of this article used to be on the JKS website. Sadly, though, information on Asai Sensei is no longer promoted or emphasized by the JKS, and this translation of the article has been removed from the website, so it is extremely difficult for non-Japanese-speaking practitioners to find. Below is the section of the article that is relevant to *tenketsu* techniques:

What is *Tenketsu Jutsu*?

Asai Sensei's technique is very deep. One example of the depth of his knowledge is in his understanding and application of the *tenketsu jutsu*. *Tenketsu jutsu* is the techniques of attacking vital points (acupressure points) on the body. In China these points have been used for generations in martial arts, *chigong* and holistic medicine. In karate, however, there are some points that holistic medicine is not aware of. In martial arts, attacking the vital points can cause fainting and numbness and inflict paint on your opponent. He learned this technique in China. These techniques were not taught openly, due to their dangerous outcome; however, we asked Asai Sensei to give us a special introduction and explanation of these techniques.

In the human body there are 365 joints, 72 "numbness points," which can cause paralysis, and 36 points which cause death. In addition to this, you must know that there is blood and chi (energy) circulating in the body. With this said, now we can introduce to you this technique. If you attack with your finger a certain point at a cer-

tain time, the circulation of both blood and chi will stop, causing numbness or death to your opponent. Also, from long ago human beings have had natural biorhythms. Everyone wakes up in the morning, sleeps at night, eats when they are hungry. Depending on the time of day, the blood circulation can vary. Therefore, when you attack a certain point at a certain time, with a certain amount of strength, you interrupt the human biorhythm. And then, just like you turn off a switch, the body rhythm is turned off, and that point of the body starts to decay. The outcome of the attack depends on the strength of the attack.

To the lack of luck of some people, including martial arts competitors, this type of attack can occur during normal training or at competitions, having the same deadly results without the real intention of the attacker. From a nonmedical point of view, this outcome is simply due to the fact that the competitor or trainee was hit at a certain point on his body at a certain time of day, which caused the interruption of the normal flow of blood and chi in his or her body. This can also happen to an unlucky person walking down the street who accidentally slips and falls, hitting the ground with certain strength, hitting a certain point in his body at a certain time, making him or her unable to move.

In addition, the opposite of this is also true, where this theory can be used for healing if you study it.

However, it is important to point out that the study of *tenketsu jutsu* can be extremely dangerous. In the past this knowledge had been kept secret, only taught to a select few. Its name had often been changed to perpetuate its secrecy.

If you want to study *tenketsu jutsu*, you must first study the following 8 points.

1. One must know where the pressure points are (the places and organs they are connected to).
2. One must know blood and chi circulation pathways and biorhythms.
3. One must know *tenketsu jutsu* theory.
4. One must study finger techniques. (*Tenketsu jutsu* mainly uses finger strikes.)
5. One must master finger-striking techniques.
6. One must train one's vision. (You must train to detect the pressure points of your moving target in the dark.)
7. One must be able to attack from a long distance.
8. One must learn how to attack, even when the outline of one's opponent is not clear, or when something is in between you and the opponent.

Of course, even if one's opponent moves, one must find the pressure points even in the dark. By merely using one's eyes, this is very difficult; therefore, one must use all one's senses to find the target. In order to perfect this, Asai Sensei made a life-size model of a person and marked all the vital points on it. Using this he was able to practise *tenketsu jutsu* from a variety of angles and positions, using not only his eyes but his whole consciousness. In addition to that, he uses the shortest and fastest way to hit his target. During karate demonstrations, Asai Sensei does not hit these vital points, but instead he hits muscle areas on the body of his demonstration subject.

If you perform the *tenketsu jutsu* technique on an opponent and use only one finger, you will hurt yourself eventually because of overusing your finger. Therefore, to maximize the efficiency of your finger attack, you must know when your opponent is at their weakest moment so that you would not have to utilize much force. Therefore, you must be able to catch the moment when your opponent is at their weakest point. You have to get the maximum effect using the minimum amount of power.

For example, when humans inhale, they are at a weak moment. If you notice, a good attack is performed at the moment of exhalation. Therefore, attacking your opponent at their moment of inhalation will require less strength and power from the attacker and still result in maximum effect.

When you attack the pressure points, don't just strike, but also twist your strike 45 degrees clockwise or vibrate your finger at the moment of impact. You can choose from a variety of techniques depending on the point you are attacking and the outcome you desire (strong, weak, deep, or shallow).

Mr. Asai says that *tenketsu jutsu* not only has techniques for attacking vital points but also has methods for attacking the pathways that connect these vital points. The center of the front part of the body is called *nimyaku*. The center of the back of the body is called *tokumyaku*. Using the knife edge (*shuto*) of the hand and the forearm of your hand (*naiwan*), you can cut the line of chi and blood circulation.

Review

Tenketsu jutsu technique believes that the human body has a pathway of chi flowing down the center of the body. This is called the *nimyaku*. It is also believed that there is a pathway of chi flowing down the back called the *tokumyaku*. If these lines are attacked, then it is easy to stop the biorhythms and circulation of one's opponent. This can be done with a *shuto* or a cutting action with the open hand.

I believe that article in 2002 was the first time he announced publicly that he practiced *tenketsu jutsu*. Let me now share the experience I had with Asai Sensei in 2004 with this very interesting and unique technique of his.

During the several years before his passing in 2006, I used to visit him monthly and had many meetings with Sensei in his office in Shinbashi (two stations away from Tokyo Station). We talked about many subjects, not only about karate but also about various cultures and the nature of people. He was interested in how people think and why they act the way they do. He said he was never interested in business and making money. He was interested in psychology, sociology, and even history. If he had not taken up karate, he could have become a school teacher.

We expanded our talk to the differences between the Japanese and the Chinese. He had a great respect for Chinese culture and what it had to offer. He said he had learned a lot when he was living in Taiwan in his early days of training. He had been sent there by the JKA just as Kanazawa, Nishiyama, and Okazaki were sent to the U.S. and Enoeda, Kase, and Shirai were sent to Europe.

He met his future wife while he was living in Taiwan. Her brother, Mr. Chen, happened to be a kung fu master of the White Crane style. Mrs. Asai told me many stories about her brother and Sensei exchanging different techniques. This process made his karate very unique, and I am sure many readers already know about this.

Though he did not tell me exactly where and from whom he learned this art, he certainly knew the technique as he demonstrated it on me. I cannot remember exactly what day it was, but it was during the winter of 2004 as I had my suit on and was carrying my overcoat. Here is a summary of the extraordinary experience I encountered on that day.

As usual, I visited his business office in Shinbashi, near Tokyo Station, one morning. Asai seemed to have a special interest in Latin America, and he always wanted to know how the JKS was doing in Latin American countries. So, I gave him the update as quickly as possible since I had to leave in one hour because of my other appointments. I wanted to finish the update quickly so that I would have time to ask him some questions.

On that day, I wanted to ask him about *tenketsu* as I had gotten a hold of a copy of the February 2002 issue of *Karate Do* in which he was featured a few weeks before my visit to Japan, and the article mentioned his ability in *kyushojutsu*, or *tenketsu*. I knew that there were some critical points in our body and that hitting such points was effective. However, I was skeptical about techniques such as para- lyzing or hurting someone with a small tap or a light grab or pinch.

I had to be frank and express my skepticism to him. He said with a little smile, "So, you are a nonbeliever." He laughed and continued, "You've come all the way from California. Let me give you a little demonstration." This was exactly what I wanted but did not expect him to offer it. So, I quickly said yes, but, right after that, I regretted it a little. A thought went through my head very quickly: *Oh no, this will be painful.*

With a smile, he told me to take off my jacket. He said, "I can do it with your jacket on, but it will be easier without it." I was nervous, but I did not want to show my fear, so I followed his direction. He said, "OK, first let's shake hands." I was not sure why he wanted to do this, so I simply extended my right hand. Instead of grabbing my hand, he quickly pinched me between my thumb and index finger. The pain was indescribable. He had total control over me with his two fingers. He raised his hand high, lowered it, and dragged me around the room at will and with ease. I simply could not do anything but follow him. I was impressed but fig-

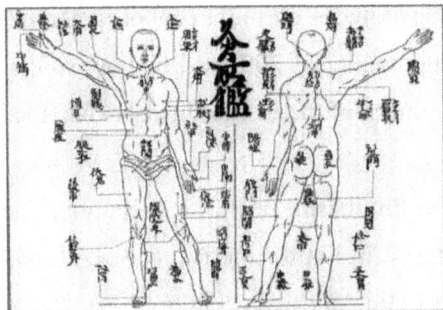

ured that anyone could do the same if he could pinch very hard. Asai knew what I was thinking, so he said with a smile, "I know anyone can do this and that it's only a parlor trick," and then continued, "Let me show you the real thing."

I was a little scared, but I was more curious about what I would experience. He told me to stand and relax. He faced me, extended both of his arms toward my face, and put his hands on my shoulders. I was nervous, so he smiled and said, "Relax! This time it will not hurt you."

He told me to bring my arms up and then down, so I did that, wondering what it was for. Then, I felt pressure on my neck. With his right hand, he was holding my left shoulder, and with his left hand, he was pressing on the right side of my neck. One of the fingers of his left hand pressed a little harder on my neck, so I felt a very small pain there, like a needle prick.

He told me to lift my arms up again, so I tried. Would you believe that I could not do it? Not only could I not move my arms, but I could not turn my head, either. My upper body was frozen, or locked. It is hard to describe exactly how my body felt at that moment. I felt no pain, and I could move my fingers and my lower body. I could see and talk, but I had no control from the neck down to the elbows. It felt as though my shoulder joints were locked and part of my body was in a cast.

I told him I could not move. He said, "Yes, that is exactly what this technique would do." He then said with a somber face, "Come back tomorrow, and I will fix you then." Even though I suspected he was just joking, I went into a small panic. Can you imagine trying to conduct a business meeting in this condition? It was not funny at all, so I begged Sensei to put me back to normal. This time he smiled and asked, "Are you sure?" So, I told him, "Most definitely yes!"

Now, I think it was interesting how he set me back. Instead of pressing my neck again, he used both open hands and very quickly hit my shoulders, sides, and arms several times. It was like having the air pounded out of my body. He did this a few times, and the pounding itself was pretty hard. The middle of my neck and shoulder muscles had some jerks and spasms, and then I got my mobility back.

Apparently, there are two kinds of *tenketsu* techniques. One is soft, which is what he demonstrated. It is called *soft* because the technique is based not on hitting a body part but rather on pressing with the fingers or different parts of the hand. When a finger is used, there are also various methods. When he pressed my neck, he used his fingertips, but I hear that, just like in karate techniques, different knuckles are also used, depending on the parts of the body a technique is applied to. The other kind is better known and is applied by hitting with many different parts of the hand or arm.

Asai said that the most important thing for a striking technique to be effective was not its power but rather the exact spot and angle of its application. He said he needed to be very careful when he gave a demonstration at a tournament. He was well known for the whipping-hand technique that he used in his *shuto* and *teisho*. When he performed, he was really hitting the opponent in the neck and the groin area. Of course, we all know that he needed to be careful with the groin area, but he said he had to be more careful with the neck area as he could literally knock the demo partner unconscious or paralyze him permanently if he applied it a certain way.

He also strengthened his fingertips by thrusting them into a bowl of sand and beans. With his one-finger jab, he could blind you, of course, but he also told me that he could hit a *tenketsu* point to cause great pain and even paralysis, temporary or permanent. I did not experience the hard *tenketsu* techniques, but I certainly did not volunteer for them, either.

I, of course, wanted to learn this technique, but he told me that it was too dangerous to pass on. He told me that he had not found anyone trustworthy enough to hand it down to. That was in 2004, two years before his passing.

He also did not have an *uchideshi* (内弟子, 'private apprentice'), though a few people wrongfully claim to have been his apprentices. He told me several times that he had not accepted any Japanese *uchideshi* and certainly not any foreign practitioners. Consequently, I must come to the very unfortunate conclusion that this art was never handed down by him to anyone. Whether you wish to believe in it or call it *mumbo jumbo*, all I can tell you is that, just like many of the *kata* he created, his *tenketsu* technique left with him when he passed in 2006.

押忍

Fusen Jisho (不戦而勝, 'not fighting results in victory')
Fusen: 'not fighting'; *ji*: 'thus'; *sho*: 'victory'

EPILOGUE
エピローグ

THE LAST SAMURAI
最後の侍

Lineup in Los Cabos, Mexico, with Asai Sensei out front and the author seated second from the right in the first row

I would like to share a picture of Asai Sensei during the final overseas seminar he held in 2006. This was taken in early July, approximately one month before his passing on August 15. You may be shocked by this picture if you happen to have known Asai Sensei and are familiar with how he looked. Indeed, he looks very thin and sickly here. He was always a thin and fit person, but he lost more than twenty pounds (ten kilograms) after a major surgery in the winter of that year. He was barely over eighty-five pounds (around forty kilograms) in this picture. I debated whether I should include this as we want to remember Asai Sensei as a healthy and active *karateka*. In the end, I decided to show this picture to the public as I feel it is my obligation to share the story of what actually happened here.

I was the coordinator and organizer of the seminar in 2006, so I know the whole story behind this last trip Sensei took. This seminar was planned for the end of June and beginning July, during which he would travel all the way to New York and then on to Los Cabos, Mexico. The big mystery of this trip is that no one can answer the following question: why did he take such a long journey that would certainly take his life?

Prior to the trip, his doctor advised him not to go. After learning this in mid-June, I immediately canceled the seminar. So, Sensei could have rested at home, and I am sure that would have added many months, and possibly years, to his life. But, he did not. Why? It is my wish to reveal this story so that his actions will not remain a mystery.

Sensei was an awesome figure when he was in his prime, just as many other JKA instructors were. But, he was different from the others, and I can tell you he was one of a kind. By reading this story, the reader will discover why I call him

The Last Samurai.

Let us travel back to June of 2006. I made another monthly business visit to Tokyo in the middle of that month. I was working for a U.S. software firm, selling an IT solution to utility companies like Tokyo Electric and Tokyo Gas. So, the job brought me back to Japan almost every month, and I certainly took advantage of this to visit Sensei. The company never knew this, but I used to check his availability in advance and then schedule my trip to Japan on the days when he would be in town.

It was a hot and humid day in June when I visited Sensei's office in Shinbashi, in the center of Tokyo. It was raining as we were in the middle of *tsuyu* (梅雨, 'rainy season'). I was supposed to wear a tie, but I remember carrying it in my briefcase as it was too humid to wear it. I always visited him at his business office because he was available to meet me one-on-one. It was impossible to do so at his dojo in Sugamo, on the outskirts of Tokyo. Sensei never gave a private lesson to anyone, so it was always in the form of a business meeting when I visited him.

We would meet in a conference room and talk as long as he was available, sometimes for hours. He had a small trading firm that was involved in commodity trading between Taiwan and Japan. He was the *shacho*, (社長, 'president'), but he told me he had nothing to do except put his seal on some of the documents. He was quite free in the mornings, so I used to visit his office at 9:00 or 10:00 AM.

I visited his office one Monday morning in June and, strangely, I missed him. His secretary told me that he'd had to go to the hospital for a checkup that day, so he had suddenly become unavailable. This was very unusual, so I asked her if he was OK. I knew he'd had major surgery in the winter, so I suspected something bad. She said, "No, he went to the doctor to get approval for the upcoming overseas trip." This was the U.S./Mexico seminar that I was hosting.

I only knew that his doctor had prohibited him from taking an overseas trip that would require long flights, time differences, changes in weather, etc. I did not know he was still so sick, so I told her that we were happy to postpone or cancel the seminar, which was scheduled for the last week of June and the first week of July.

The *dan* exam in Los Cabos, Mexico

She said that would be a good idea as she did not think he was in good enough condition to take a two-week seminar trip to the Americas. I told her that I would come back on the following day just to give Sensei my respects and an update on my activities in the U.S. In fact, that very night I called my contacts in three different locations (New York, Texas, and Los Cabos) to inform them of my decision to postpone the seminar. After learning of Sensei's condition, all three contacts understood the situation and gladly accepted my decision.

I visited his office the next morning and found him there. He was wearing a suit and tie, which he always did at his office. I used to tell him he looked very professional, but he would come back with a joke, saying, "I hate this monkey suit, but I have to wear it. Otherwise, the guests think I am just a janitor," and he would then laugh out loud.

So, that morning he was dressed well, as usual, but I was shocked when I saw him for two reasons. One was that he had lost more weight in the one or two months prior. He was a thin person anyway, weighing less than 130 pounds (60 kilograms), but what I saw on that day was a skin-and-bones figure of Sensei. I said to myself, *My God, what happened to him?* As he sat there with his back straight, he was swaying slightly, which had never happened before.

The second reason for my surprise was his look. He looked extremely upset and almost angry. Of course, I did not know why. I never would have imagined that he was upset with me, so I thought he had just had a bad day.

During the usual greeting, he said nothing, which was unusual. After my greeting, I started to tell him that we were happy to postpone the seminar and that the three contacts in the U.S. and Mexico were in full agreement with me. At that moment, he almost screamed at me, "Who decided to postpone it?"

I said, "I did when I heard about your condition."

He told me with a much quieter but more authoritative voice, "This is *my* health, and *I* know best. You must not make decisions regarding my trip and seminar."

I quickly apologized for having made a decision without consulting him, but I was very much convinced that I had made the right decision, so I continued, saying, "Asai Sensei, we are not canceling the event. We will do this in the fall, when the weather is better. You seem to have lost a lot of weight, so please gain some back and rest during the hot summer. You will be in better shape to take a long trip to the U.S. Besides, all of us will worry about your health if you visit us now."

I thought my comments made much sense as we were concerned about his health first. He came back to me with the same authoritative way of talking, "I have agreed to visit the U.S. and Mexico. When I make a commitment, I always deliver. If you cancel or change this trip, I will never visit you again."

Well, what could I say to this statement? I told him I understood and that we would hold the seminar according to the original plan. But, I told him we would do it under one condition. I asked him to bring at least one assistant instructor with him so that he could watch over him during his trip to the U.S. I wanted to travel with him, but my work appointments were already set for the following week, so it was impossible to do so.

He agreed to my request. The assistant instructors were also concerned about the overseas trip and were against the idea, so two of them volunteered to accompany him. I felt a little more comfortable knowing that two young guys were going to be tagging along so that Sensei would not need to carry his bag or walk much as they told me that they would get a wheelchair at the airport.

I called my three contacts that night and told them that we needed to forget the postponement and that we would maintain the original plan. They were very happy as the seminar was only one or two weeks away, and it would have been very difficult to change the dates and rebook the training sites. They would have had fewer participants, too, if we had changed the dates. They were also happy that two more

Japanese instructors would be with Sensei.

The final seminar in New York

The Asai party took off from Japan as originally scheduled, and their first destination was New York City. I really wanted to join them but, due to my work schedule, could not do so. I called the host and spoke with the assistant instructors to check on Sensei. They told me that he was OK after the flight, so I was relieved at this news as I was worried about the long flight from Tokyo to New York. At the end of that week, they would fly to Los Angeles to meet me. Then, we would fly to the final destination, Los Cabos, Mexico, together.

I took a few days off from work and joined them at LAX on Thursday to spend the long weekend with them. When I saw him at LAX, he looked very weak and tired. The assistant instructors told me that his condition had gotten worse as they had traveled from New York to Houston and Los Angeles on the way to Los Cabos, which is located on the Baja California Peninsula, west of mainland Mexico.

It was obvious that the fatigue was wearing him down. He went to bed as soon as we arrived at the hotel. It was a good thing that we had a full day to rest. He was in bed almost all day but got up and joined us at dinner. At lunchtime on Saturday, we went to his room and found him in bed. He told us that he could not get up on his own. We had to help him sit up first. He was totally exhausted and too weak to stand up.

We were so worried about his health that we called the local doctor to have him give him a quick examination. The doctor came and told us that he must

The final seminar in Los Cabos, Mexico

not be moved. He needed to rest until his departure date on Monday if he wanted to go home then. When the translator, a representative of the JKS in Los Cabos, told him what the doctor had said, Sensei said he would rest in the afternoon but that he was determined to go to the training site that evening. After hearing this reply, the doctor said he would not guarantee his life if he did this. Sensei said it was OK even if he died during the seminar. The doctor gave him a few shots as he was getting weak and dehydrated and left the room, shaking his head in disbelief at his patient.

That evening it took almost one hour for him to get ready to leave for the training session. We had to hold him as he tried to walk from his room to the car. At the training site, he was too weak to teach the class, so he let one of his assistants run it. He sat in a chair for a few hours, all throughout both classes we had that night. However, he forced himself to be at the front of the lineup.

He showed commitment in visiting and teaching his karate. He also knew that he would not have been able to visit the U.S. and Mexico if he had postponed it. He knew this trip was not good for his health, but he wanted to do it. He did the same thing on Sunday and left us on Monday. We traveled together to Los Angeles, where we separated. As he

Departure, Los Cabos International Airport

slowly walked to his plane, I bowed deeply to show him my respect for having shown me dedication and true commitment.

I heard that he did not rest after returning to Japan as he participated in the All Japan Championship at the end of July despite everyone's asking him to skip it so that he could rest. He watched all the events and then collapsed immediately afterward. At that point, he went into a coma and never regained consciousness until his passing on August 15.

I knew he was in the hospital, so I called his office almost daily in August. I was hoping he would regain consciousness and his health, but that did not happen. He did not give his body enough rest and was running his life faster than what his body could keep up with. When I made a call to his office on August 15, the secretary gave me the shocking news of his passing. He was only seventy-one years old.

We needed him for many more years. He had too many things to pass down to his students, but now he is gone forever. I learned about thirty Asai Ryu *kata* from him, but he knew and practiced over a hundred *kata*; thus, the majority of the Asai Ryu *kata* might have died with him. Besides his *kata*, there are other arts that were lost, as well. I discussed his expertise in *tenketsu jutsu* in the last chapter, and he was also an expert in several weapons, such as the *bo*, nunchaku (ヌンチャク), and *kyusetsuben* (九節鞭, 'nine-section whip'). These are also gone with him.

When I received this painful news on August 15, I must confess that I experienced a serious feeling of guilt. I thought to myself, *He could have lived longer if I had not invited him this summer*, and, *I really should have postponed that seminar even if he got angry with me and kicked me out of his office. Then, he might still be alive.* This thought stayed on my mind every day and haunted me terribly.

A few months later, I had a chance to visit his house on the outskirts of Tokyo to pay my respects to his widow. As is Japanese tradition, she had a portable home shrine to Sensei, to which I prayed and apologized.

Funeral in Tokyo, September 2006

I spent a few hours talking to Mrs. Asai, during which I apologized to her. She was surprised and asked why. I spent some minutes explaining why I felt deep regret and blamed myself for what had happened to Sensei. I was overwhelmed with emotion as tears rolled out of my eyes.

Upon seeing this, she probably felt sorry for me as she told me that I could not have changed anything even if I had tried. She said, "Yokota Sensei, do not blame yourself. No one could have changed the outcome. I know that once my husband made a decision, no one could change his mind. He was not afraid of dying, and he loved his karate more than his life.

Asai Sensei's grave in Tokyo

I suspect he actually wanted to die on the training floor in New York City." She brought me closure. I no longer have to feel guilty for inviting Sensei to the U.S. and hosting the event that definitely shortened his life.

Now I believe that he most likely thought it would have been not only acceptable but desirable to have died in the U.S. or Mexico while he was giving his last seminar. I am afraid most senior instructors in Japan have lost honor and the samurai spirit. They would not risk their life in teaching karate and cannot show samurai spirit. Many of them are more interested in making money and increasing their political power.

Asai Sensei demonstrated samurai spirit even though it shortened his life. He showed us that he would keep his promise and teach *karatedo* until the last days of his life. As far as I am concerned, I do not see anyone else in the Shotokan world who is like him. This is why I say he was the last samurai.

I am truly honored that I could be there with him at his last seminar. All those who were at the Los Cabos training in 2006 must consider themselves to be very lucky to have been able to experience a samurai deed by the greatest master of Shotokan, who was indeed the last samurai.

押忍

Tenth *dan* diploma awarded by the JKS in 2006

His nickname, *Thunderstorm*, will live forever.

Lightning Source UK Ltd.
Milton Keynes UK
UKOW06f2113231017
311525UK00008B/1023/P

9 780998 223605